Carolina of Orange-Nassau

Ancestress of the royal houses of Europe

Carolina of Orange-Nassau

Ancestress of the royal houses of Europe

Moniek Bloks

Winchester, UK
Washington, USA

First published by Chronos Books, 2019
Chronos Books is an imprint of John Hunt Publishing Ltd., No. 3 East St., Alresford,
Hampshire SO24 9EE, UK
office1@jhpbooks.net
www.johnhuntpublishing.com

For distributor details and how to order please visit the 'Ordering' section on our website.

Text copyright: Moniek Bloks 2018

ISBN: 978 1 78535 914 9
978 1 78535 915 6 (ebook)
Library of Congress Control Number: 2017960099

A CIP catalogue record for this book is available from the British Library.

Design: Stuart Davies

Printed and bound by CPI Group (UK) Ltd, Croydon, CR0 4YY, UK

We operate a distinctive and ethical publishing philosophy in
all areas of our business, from our global network of authors to
production and worldwide distribution.

Contents

Acknowledgements

I would like to thank my parents, Jos and Karin, and my sister Anouk for their support and understanding. I would also like to thank the Royal Archives and His Majesty King Willem-Alexander for allowing me access to Carolina's letters.

Introduction

The name Carolina of Orange-Nassau will not be a household name for many people. This appears to be the case with many women in history. Carolina was the eldest surviving child of William IV, Prince of Orange and Anne of Hanover, and therefore the only sibling of William V, Prince of Orange. When her father was named stadtholder Carolina was his only child and so the stadtholdership was made hereditary in the female line. The birth of her little brother ended the possibility that Carolina would inherit the stadtholdership but she remained his heir until he had heirs of his own. During the last months of William's minority, a heavily pregnant Carolina acted as his regent.

Carolina inherited a love of music and a talent for it as well from her mother and after her marriage to the German Prince Charles Christian of Nassau-Weilburg, she brought the nine-year-old prodigy Mozart to The Hague. He returned to her court many years later as an adult, grateful that Carolina's personal physician had saved not only his life but also that of his sister. Carolina loved music but she was pregnant for most of her married life and sometimes she found that her pregnancies hindered her musical hobby. She was very much attached to her children and was devastated at the loss of her first two sons. Eventually, she would face the loss of over half of her children. Despite these losses, she remained strong.

Above all, Carolina loved her little brother. They had an age difference of five years, but they were orphaned at a young age and the pair were unusually close. During her lifetime, Carolina wrote to her brother every few days with a few interruptions when she was pregnant or giving birth. She continued to long for the Netherlands and especially her favourite palace, the Loo Palace. She never lived to see her little brother banished from his country and she would have been proud to see her nephew return to the Netherlands to become its first King in 1815.

Carolina was Dutch through and through, despite her English mother and her marriage to a German Prince. Her heart never left the Netherlands. Until 1922, Carolina's heirs were still mentioned in the Dutch constitution with the possibility of inheriting the Dutch crown. Her many children and grandchildren spread out across the thrones of Europe and Carolina is the ancestress of all the ruling Kings and Queens of Europe, including the Netherlands. A biography of this musical and loving woman 275 years after her birth only seems right.

Chapter 1

Birth and Youth

Princess Wilhelmine Carolina of Orange-Nassau was born on 28 February 1743 at the Princely Court of Leeuwarden as the eldest surviving child of the Stadtholder of Friesland, Groningen, Drenthe and Gelderland, William IV, Prince of Orange and Anne of Hanover, also known as Anne, Princess Royal.

Her father was the de facto head of state as the Stadtholder of Friesland, Groningen, Drenthe and Gelderland, which were all provinces in the Dutch Republic. This was a largely hereditary role, which he had been born to fulfil as he was born six weeks after his father's death. His father, Johan William Friso, head of the Frisian branch of the House of Orange-Nassau, had drowned in the Hollands Diep as he was travelling to The Hague on 22 October 1751. He was just 23-years-old. The title itself originated from the middle ages and became closely associated with the Republic of the Seven United Netherlands. Some provinces refused to appoint a stadtholder during two occasions, which became known as the First and Second Stadtholderless Period. Previous stadtholders include William the Silent, leader of the Dutch revolt against Spanish rule, his sons Philip William, Maurice and Frederick Henry, William II and William III, who also became King William III of England, Scotland and Ireland. In addition, her father was Prince of Orange, a title associated with the Principality of Orange in Southern France. Although the Principality itself was ceded to King Louis XIV of France in 1713, the title continued to be used.

Her mother was the eldest daughter of King George II of Great Britain and Caroline of Ansbach and she was thus known as the Princess Royal, an honorific title for the eldest daughter of the King. She was born on 2 November 1709 in Herrenhausen

3

Palace in Hanover, five years before her paternal grandfather would succeeded as King George I of Great Britain. She was named for the Queen her grandfather would succeed, Anne, Queen of Great Britain, the last of the Protestant Stuarts. Anne had been pregnant many times but only one child survived past infancy, Prince William, Duke of Gloucester. He tragically died at the age of 11 in 1700. As Parliament did not wish the throne to revert to a Catholic, most notably Anne's half-brother James Francis Edward Stuart, also known as the Old Pretender, the Act of Settlement 1701 settled the succession on Sophia of Hanover, a granddaughter of James VI and I, and her Protestant heirs. Sophia died shortly before Queen Anne did and so her son succeeded as King George I.

The marriage between the Prince of Orange and the daughter of the British King was perhaps not one many would expect. However, the Hanoverians were relatively unpopular and a marriage with a Protestant Prince would be popular and perhaps one day, the Prince of Orange would play a large role in the Dutch Republic. The marriage was also meant to improve the relationship between the Dutch Republic and England, which had been bad since the War of the Spanish Succession.[1]

Her parents had married on 7 March 1734 in St. James's Chapel. Her mother had spent much time studying Dutch history and copying works by Titian and Van Dyck from the Royal Collection.[2] Anne walked down the aisle in a wedding dress of stiff blue French silk, embroidered with thread. It was lavishly trimmed with ruffles of fine lace and loops of diamonds. She wore her robe of state over it and her six-foot-train was supported by eight peers' daughters who were dressed in white and silver. Around her neck was a magnificent diamond necklace, which had been a gift from her future husband. The ceremony was rather quick and from Lord Hervey's[3] memoirs we learn that the ceremony was "more like the mournful pomp of a sacrifice than the celebration of marriage and put one in mind rather of an

4

Iphigenia leading to the altar than of a bride."[4] It seemed like an auspicious start to the marriage and the reaction to the Prince of Orange was rather lukewarm.

However, Anne was smitten with her new husband. After a brief honeymoon at Kew, the couple returned to the court of Anne's father. Lord Hervey again comments on the situation, "She always behaved to him as if he was an Adonis and he hardly took any notice of her at all nor gave her one look by which one could have guessed that they ever slept in the same sheets."[5] Despite the lukewarm reception, William was given the Order of the Garter and Parliament made him a British subject. Soon the couple would be on their way to the Netherlands. Anne was given a pair of diamond pendant earrings by her father and her mother later agonised over her departure, "Dear Hart, my sadness is indescribable. I never had any sorrows over you Anne, this is the first cruel one. Caroline behaves so well but our conversations always finish on the same sad note. The King, who sends you affectionate greetings, is worse than us all. To change the conversation I was forced to talk about Griff. Orange is good man and will ever be a great favourite of mine...love me always as tenderly as the most affectionate mother flatters herself that you do."[6]

The party left from Gravesend and after a calm journey across the North Sea, they landed at Rotterdam. They would then need to cross the Zuiderzee to Friesland, where William's mother anxiously awaited them. Marie Louise of Hesse-Kassel had been informed that Anne, as the daughter of a King, must take precedence over her, but Marie Louise needn't be told. She had already moved out of the Court when William had come of age and now lived in the next street over. Although Anne seized the first opportunity she could to return to England she refers to him in her letters as "Pepin" or "Pip", while he responds with "my adorable Annin."[7]

Anne was soon pregnant with her first child and William

was absolutely delighted. He wrote to her that her pregnancy, "serves but to redouble and augment if that were possible my love and my devotion for you, my incomparable Annin."[8] Anne was in London at the time and she became ill on the ship back to the Netherlands, forcing it back to port. William was not amused and he ordered her back at once. She finally arrived at Calais and the couple travelled to The Hague to celebrate the New Year and to await the child.

Although Anne grew bigger or as William wrote to his mother, "she gets heavier and less inclined to move about."[9], rumours soon began to grow that there was no pregnancy at all. Anne had informed her husband of her pregnancy in July 1734 but by the next spring even William had become agitated. By 20 April 1735 it appeared that there would be no child. William wrote, "I can hardly bear to tell you but the accoucheur has told her that there is no child. It is not the fact that she is not pregnant which gives me pain we are both young and if it not to be this year then we dare to hope for another time and besides it is the will of God...it is the blow to my poor princess which is so terrible. The swelling stays with her though the doctors assure me that there is no danger."[10]

We will probably never know what exactly ailed the Princess, but in the summer of 1736 Anne announced another pregnancy. The child was due in December and this time they were sure it was a real pregnancy, which may account for the late announcement. Her labour began on 3 December 1736 and she was assisted by a male midwife, Dr. Sands, who had been sent over from England by Anne's mother. It would end in tragedy. The child was too large to be expelled naturally and after four days of labour Anne's life was in danger. Dr. Sands was forced to kill the baby to save the mother. It was a baby girl, who lay in state for three days before being interred in the New Church at Delft. Anne wasn't able to leave her bed until Christmas day. Anne's mother wrote to her, "words cannot tell how I have suffered and my joy at receiving you back from God. I have you and that is enough. May he grant you renewed strength and make a happy mother of a family, be certain that you will have happier and easier labours than this in the future. May God give you every blessing and you will not lack it mein liebes kind (my darling child) if you submit yourself entirely to his will."[11] In February 1737 the couple left The Hague and Anne appeared to be in good condition. She was certainly well enough to spend the summer travelling. The year would end in another tragedy for Anne, as her mother died after an agonising time in her sickbed on 20 November 1737.

Anne was probably pregnant again in 1738, but it must have ended in tragedy as it was suddenly no longer reported upon, until the announcement of a new pregnancy in October 1739. On Christmas Eve it was recorded, "on the evening of 23rd December Madame the Princess of Orange Nassau was delivered of a young Princess in whom the light of life never shone."[12] It must have been one of the lowest points in Anne's life.

It would be another three years before Anne could at last celebrate the birth of a child who would live. Carolina was the child who survived. She was baptised Wilhelmina Carolina in the Grote Kerk in Leeuwarden on 10 March 1743. It was upon the wish of Anne's father that the child was named after his beloved wife, Caroline of Ansbach and Anne's mother. "His Majesty, the King himself, wishes to be the Godfather of the Princess who has just been born, and is named Caroline. I am glad to communicate to you his orders, since the manner in which the king does so adds to the good news."[13] Anne had no problem to abide by her father's wishes. She had just seen her life's wish fulfilled, she had given birth to a living child.

Her grandmother Marie Louise acted as her godmother and carried her to the font. William was overjoyed at the birth of Carolina and seemed to care little that she was not the hoped for boy. Anne fed Carolina herself and she recovered quickly from the birth, which must have been great, considering her previous childbirths. She received letters of congratulations from her sisters and her brother Frederick, the Prince of Wales.

When Carolina was five months old, her father wrote proudly from the Loo Palace in Apeldoorn, "everyone is surprised to find little Caroline so robust and advanced."[14] Anne went to visit her sister Mary in Kassel. Mary had married the Landgrave Frederick of Hesse-Kassel in 1740 and had just given birth to her second son, William, in June. Her first son, another William, had died in infancy the year before. By September Anne and Carolina were travelling to Oranienstein as William took a cure in Ems for stomach problems. She wrote of Carolina, "there has never been a child so easy to wean and she sleeps elevens hours a night."[15] They returned to Leeuwarden to celebrate Carolina's first Christmas.

By early February 1745 it became clear that Anne was pregnant again. It was a difficult pregnancy and by March William was writing to his mother that she had had a bleeding. A midwife confirmed that she had had a miscarriage but a doctor from Leiden disagreed. Two weeks later he had to admit that the midwife was right. Anne had lost the child. For the latter part of 1745 William was away to Frankfurt for the imperial election where Maria Theresa of Austria's husband Francis of Lorraine was elected Holy Roman Emperor. Anne wrote to William many times and included of little Carolina, "she looks for you everywhere with a melancholy air, and ask all the time where you are."[16] He returned to Anne and Carolina at the Loo Palace in November, where they were visited by William, Count Bentinck who wrote, "The Princess Royal is in very good health and most excellent spirits and always equally cheerful. Princess Caroline is the finest strongest child of her age I ever saw and Loo is one of the finest situated houses I know."[17] When he brought Carolina a present of china, she "made me eat part of her dinner..."[18]

On 15 November 1746 Anne gave birth to a second daughter who was christened Anna Maria, for her mother and grandmother.

Tragically Anna Maria would die just over a month later on 29 December 1746 and William was devastated. He incoherently wrote, "this special and dear (baby) we hope she will find peace and that one day we shall be reunited."[19] Anne, faced with yet another loss, broke down completely. Reportedly she wept day and night and "her milk is still plentiful, which makes things worse."[20]

She was depressed throughout the winter and devoted herself to little Carolina. She was in regular contact with her sister Amalia, who tried to lift her spirits. While mourning for their lost baby William and Anne finally got the restoration they had wished for. William was at last elected Captain-General and Stadtholder of all seven of the United Provinces. "God give us the strength and ability to bear this burden", her father had responded upon hearing the news.[21]

To celebrate, William, Anne and Carolina toured the canals of Amsterdam in a glass-topped boat at night. Crowds filled the streets to see the family and fireworks were set off. Two days later, they arrived in The Hague for their installation. There was now also added pressure of ensuring the line of succession. The stadtholdership of the provinces was made hereditary for the Frisian princes of the House of Orange-Nassau and was also extended to include the female line, so that little Carolina could succeed in the event that she had no brothers.

Anne threw herself into the restoration of the official residence of the stadtholders, the Binnenhof in The Hague, which had been unused since 1702. On 9 March 1748 Anne at last gave birth to a living son in the quarters of her predecessor as Princess Royal. She was 37-years-old and this was her 7th pregnancy. William was delighted and the little Prince was created Count of Buren before the day was out. William wrote proudly to his mother, "he takes the breast though he's still a little clumsy about it, but he grows in strength and weight while we watch."[22] Fireworks were set off every day for a week and there was great rejoicing in the country. In April the little baby was simply baptised William, at the Grote Kerk in The Hague. Carolina was now displaced in the succession, but she had more serious concerns as she was suffering from measles, an often deadly illness at the time. Luckily she recovered and one of her first surviving letters was written during this time. Although most of her older letters are in French, this first surviving one is written in Dutch. She writes to her father, "Dearly beloved papa, take the time to read my letter, I hope it pleases you, my dear papa, to see me advance in this post. I am papa's obedient daughter. C. Princesse d'Orange."[23] In another letter, dated just a few days before her brother's birth she writes to her grandmother Marie Louise, "Most beloved grandmama, I have received my most pleasing present with great joy, for which I thank grandmama. I recommend myself to grandmama's thoughts. I am with love, C. Princesse d'Orange." The letter is dated 5 March 1748.[24]

On 22 April 1748, Carolina received a present of "two little African Moors and a precious hammock from that part of the word."[25] One of them was named Fortuin (Fortune) and he died a year after being presented to Carolina. It is recorded that "the little Moor of Princess Carolina" was buried in Scheveningen near The Hague on 1 February 1749. He was just 13-years-old. We don't know what happened to the other Moor.[26]

In an undated letter, probably sent not much later, Carolina writes to Marie Louise, "My little brother is very healthy and grows fast." She again thanks her grandmother for a present. Early in 1751 Carolina writes to her grandmother again, but this time she switches to French. Marie Louise must have been ill in early 1751 as Carolina wishes that she would be better soon. Again, the indulgent grandmama sends the young Princess a present. Anne made sure that Carolina and William were close, a bond that would last the rest of their lives.

William and Anne could only occassionaly escape to the Loo Palace, which they loved so much. During the hot summer of

1751 William suffered from colics and a toothache. Anne was visited by the composer Handel in the autumn, while at the Loo. In the spring of 1751, Anne received the news that her brother, Frederick, Prince of Wales had died after catching a chill.

Anne was more worried about her husband, who during the last couple of years had also had bouts of illness. In May he wrote to Anne that he had a pain in his right side which was so severe it caused him to have a facial twitch. He could hardly eat, which he blamed on the cooking and had to sleep on the ground floor, because he could not walk up the stairs. By August, he was nearly broken down. His doctors advised him to go to the spa at Aix-la-Chapelle. He set out on his 50th birthday with his personal physician. Although he despised the cures prescribed to him, he dutifully drank the ten glasses a day. Anne was left in charge at home and he wrote to her regularly, often ending with the familiar, "your Pip." Their two children also wrote to William and William wrote back to Anne, "the little one tells me he is being very good. I hope you agree."[27] Just as Carolina's father was working on improving his health, Carolina herself fell ill with a high fever. William heard the news and promptly collapsed. While little Carolina recovered, William did not. Perhaps fearing the end was near he wrote to Anne, "Farewell my dear heart, Pearl among women, my joy whom I love more every day. As God is my witness you are my life's good fortune. Know that I am your most faithful, most tender and best of friends Pepin."[28]

Anne's response is the good news that Carolina was improving. "She continues to do marvellously she had started to sleep again for twelve hours a night and gets up for an hour a day the doctors are quite astonished. I ought to be going to the Comedie tonight but a dreadful storm has stopped me so I have been singing in Carolina's room. I find as always a great void in your absence." Four weeks later the doctors were convinced that William was improving. William had had enough of Aix-la-Chapelle and returned to The Hague despite the appalling weather. He arrived at Huis Ten Bosch on 10 October with a pounding headache and an obstruction of the throat. He seemed better after a week of rest and he planned to attend church the following week. On 18 October he entered the chapel, complained of the heat and had a massive stroke. He was bled twice and was unconscious for three days. He died at two o'clock in the morning on 22 October 1751 as Anne kneeled beside him.[29] Carolina was just eight-years-old, while her brother, now the new Prince of Orange, was just three-years-old.

Carolina's mother was in a sense of disbelief. Anne went from her husband's deathbed to signing the letters of notification. Before the country was even awake, William's body was on its way to The Hague and later that day Anne was already receiving visits of condolence. Two days later, Anne was declared Governor and Guardian. An autopsy was performed on William and the results were announced publicly on 25 October. The stomach and chest appeared normal, but the brain was full of blood. His twisted backbone had pressed up against the jugular vein and the increasing curvature had blocked the blood supply to the lungs and heart. The coffin was interred in the New Church in Delft next to the tiny coffin of their first-born daughter.

Anne's regency was met with doubt. She had always been a foreigner *(The English Woman)* to the Dutch, but after twenty years in their country, she refused to let them put her down. In 1752 the Duke of Brunswick wrote to Empress Maria Theresa, "the Princess does far more work in a day than the Prince did in fourteen."[30] Anne was already proving to be an excellent regent.

Anne tried to keep family life as normal as possible after William's death. They usually spent the summer months at the Loo Palace or Soestdijk Palace and the winter months in The Hague. She seemed to get along well with Carolina, but her relationship with her strong-willed son was more difficult. A deputy from Utrecht wrote that the young Prince "did not even respect his sister", and had called her a beast.[31] There was some improvement in William's behaviour after Anne hired a French man named Joncourt as his instructor. Anne transferred her love of music to her daughter, whose playing on the harpsichord was later praised.

In June 1753 Anne and her children travelled to Leeuwarden to visit William's mother, Marie Louise, and they spent several weeks there. By then Anne's health had been slowly deteriorating, but she refused to name a regent in case she should die before her son came of age. She and Marie Louise had not always had the best of relationships, but the few weeks in Leeuwarden seemed to improve that. She also decided on the regency. If she should die before William became of age the regency was effectively split in two between Marie Louse and the Duke of Brunswick. The personal guardianship of the two children was shared between Marie Louise, the Duke of Brunswick and King George II of Great Britain. The more political role was left dormant, while the Duke of Brunswick continued in his military role as acting Captain-General.

Throughout the late 1750s Anne's health continued to decline, while the pressures of the Seven Years War increased. She soon believed herself to be dying and began to prepare herself. One of her main concerns was Carolina. Her personal wealth was already well organised and she was set to inherit lands and goods, separate from her brother. She was also slated to inherit much of Anne's dowry, which had been invested in British funds. To ensure her daughter's independence she sought a suitable marriage for her. She realised only too well that it might be left too late if William dealt with when he came of age. Several possibilities were discussed, such as her cousin Prince William Henry, later created Duke of Gloucester and Edinburgh, the son of Frederick, Prince of Wales. Anne rejected any English match. Carolina was thoroughly Dutch and she would need to remain to be seen so, as she was still the heir presumptive of her brother. By 1755 Anne had her eye on Prince Charles Christian of Nassau-Weilburg, who despite him being eight years older than Carolina, was seen as the perfect bridegroom. Anne ordered her counsellors to draw up a document with all the pros and cons concerning a possible marriage with Charles Christian. She liked him, if only for the fact that he grew up far away from court life and that he received an excellent education.[32]

Charles Christian of Nassau-Weilburg was born on 16 January 1735 as the youngest child and only son of Charles August, Prince of Nassau-Weilburg (17 September 1685 – 9 November 1753) and Auguste Friederike of Nassau-Idstein (17 August 1699 – 8 June 1750). He was educated from the age of nine in Lausanne in Switzerland by Charles de La Pottrie. He took over the administration of the principality of Weilburg in 1751 and it was in quite a good financial situation under his father's guidance. His father died in 1753 and Charles Christian became the reigning Prince of Nassau-Weilburg. His wish to meet Princess Carolina led him to the Netherlands in 1755 and to England the next year to be inspected by King George II. He liked her so well, that he made no other inquiries into the availability of other Princesses.[33] Likewise, Carolina had already settled upon no other hand than his.[34]

Charles was invited to The Hague and seemed amiable enough. Anne was delighted by him and was set on him as her daughter's future husband. She would need the permission of the States-General for any marriage for Carolina. She wrote a letter to King George II praising him to no end. There was one issue with Charles, he was a Lutheran. Any sons Carolina might have must be raised in the Reformed Church if they were to be heirs to William. Charles refused to change his faith and by the time he had been convinced to allow any children they might have to be raised in the Reformed faith, the States-General refused to discuss the marriage. In addition, if the worst happened and Carolina would be forced to succeed her brother, it would be Charles Christian who could possibly dispute his own wife's succession.[35] The financial side of things didn't look as good either. The counsellors wrote, "This marriage will put the Princess Carolina into mediocrity if she lived outside the country and would reduce her to below mediocrity if she remained there."[36] Charles Christian's finances were well below what was expected to maintain a high-born Princess of the House of Orange-Nassau. Anne knew that she would be able to supplement any financial needs with a dowry and a dotation from her own means but still negotiations dragged on for nearly three years.[37]

Anne personally wrote to the Charles Christian's father, "The gratitude which I owe you for all the care you wish to have for my children pledges me to consult Your Highness with regards to their well-being.

"It is a question of establishing my daughter; she is still very young; but the position of our House in this Republic compels me to wish that she may dwell there and have children early in order to tranquillize the good intentions and discourage those factious who are always lulled by the hope of seeing the end of the government while there are only two heads. The Prince of Nassau-Weilburg having passed here, I have had occasion to examine his conduct fairly and believe him incapable of vices, and seeking the approbation of honest men. His mediocre fortune will naturally make him more supple and more fit to live with my daughter with certain respects, and submit to many things here, which would not please a more powerful prince, so that I have given him some hopes. However, I did not want to commit myself more without sending it to you. I hope you will find that I did not say too much in his favour."[38]

By October 1758 Anne suffered continually from a heaviness in her legs and a fever. Anne desperately appealed to the Duke of Brunswick to use his influence. He advised her to appear before them and she did so, clearly very ill, on 12 December 1758. She managed to celebrate Christmas and the New Year but she woke up on 5 January with a great pain in her side. Despite her illness, young William wrote to his grandmother, "Mama continues to do well."[39] Her legs were wrapped in bandages as they continued to swell and she was placed in an armchair. With an unsteady hand she managed to sign her daughter's marriage papers, which had been brought to her. On 9 January the pain was so severe that she screamed out in pain when she tried to bend her legs. She told her servant, "I have no fear of death, I have been ready for it too long and I know where I am going. I have often prayed to God for a swift and painless death."[40] She drifted for several days between consciousness and unconsciousness. On 12 January she briefly rallied and prayed with her chaplain. She then had her son and daughter brought to her. To them she said, "May God make you as good and happy as I would wish." She added that they should look towards the Duke of Brunswick as a father. The Duke of Brunswick arrived in the nick of time and she looked to him for assurance that the marriage papers were all in order. He assured her that all was in order. Carolina supported her mother as she blessed both her and her brother. She fell into a peaceful sleep and died, as she had prayed, a painless death at 11 o'clock that night. Carolina had stayed with her mother until the very end, but William had been sent to bed. Her autopsy set the cause of death at dropsy. She also had three gallstones, an extraordinary large heart and her lungs appeared blue.

Anne, Princess Royal and Princess of Orange lay in state in the Binnenhof, like her husband before her. Despite her initial unpopularity, the crowds passing by her coffin, were far greater than those for her husband. She wore a white satin gown with frilled sleeves and a lace cap. Symbolic crowns showed her royal birth. Her funeral took place on 23 February 1759 and 11-year-old William walked as far as the city walls with the procession. She was interred next to her husband and first-born daughter in the New Church in Delft.

Marie Louise set out to fulfil Anne's dying wish. She departed for The Hague where she stayed for over three months. She met her grandchildren at Noordeinde Palace.[41] On 6 February 1759, Marie Louise wrote to the Duke of Brunswick that she was glad to hear that two provinces had given their permission for the marriage of "my darling girl Princess Carolina."[42] Even so, it would take almost another year before the marriage could go ahead. Even the Dutch people began to long for the marriage to take place. Bentinck wrote to the Duke of Brunswick in March 1759, "The inclination of the public for the conclusion of this marriage will mean that one will not want to be burdened with preventing it or delaying it ... Even in Amsterdam a very large number of the most considerable bourgeois wish it and are impatient to see that the case drags on ..."[43]

The first provinces to give their permission were Zeeland and Gelderland. Marie Louise wrote to the Duke of Brunswick, "I am delighted to learn of the resolutions of the provinces of Zeeland and Gelderland the consent of these two provinces to the marriage of my dear granddaughter. I hope that Friesland will follow closely."[44]

Marie Louise returned to Leeuwarden and was informed by Charles Christian in The Hague on 13 February 1760 that the Duke of Brunswick had informed the States-General that the marriage was to take place the next month. There were still five provinces that had not given their express permission, but they had also decided not to fight the marriage and so at last, everyone was in agreement.[45]

A very happy Charles Christian wrote to Marie Louise, "The Duke has now informed the Assembly of the States-General that the marriage which will fill my felicity is fixed at the 5th of next month. Letters of notification to the various provinces are leaving today. I can not, Madam, remain in regard to your Highness in such a happy time. The desire to make the happiness of a Princess, as amiable as she is virtuous, my gratitude to God, the gratitude which I owe to Your Highness, the plan which I form to answer all the duties which this union imposes upon me, flattering ideas that occupy me ... "[46]

Chapter 2

The Early Years of Marriage and the Regency

Carolina and Charles Christian were married on 5 March 1760 in The Hague but festivities were also held in Leeuwarden where Marie Louise presided over them. The marriage took place in the Grote Kerk in The Hague and Carolina wore a silver wedding dress set with silver fringes.[1] After the ceremony the party went to Noordeinde Palace for further celebrations. The wedding hall was decorated with famous masters and hundreds of lights. In the middle of the hall stood a large table in the shape of a double cross.[2]

On the occasion of her marriage, Carolina receive a dotation of 80.000 guilders, a marriage gift of 20.000 guilders and 10.000 guilders worth of clothing, jewellery and silver.[3] Carolina was still an important person in the succession and Charles Christian was appointed Governor of Bergen-Op-Zoom and acting Captain-General so they could settle in The Hague at the Huis Honselaarsdijk, which has now mostly disappeared. Carolina fell pregnant almost immediately after her wedding and she gave birth to her first child on 18 December 1760 between 8 and 9 in the evening. It was a boy who was named George William and the States-General acted as godparent for the young boy, giving him the name Belgicus.[4] The birth went well and Carolina recovered quickly. The boy was to be raised in "the true Christian Reformed religion"[5] and was given a dotation of 4.000 guilders a year.[6] A delighted Charles Christian wrote to the newly acceded King George III of the United Kingdom, "My wife has just been happily delivered of a son." King George responded most joyfully, "My cousin, I rejoice exceedingly at the happy delivery of my cousin, your wife, and I congratulate you most cordially on the birth of your son. I accept with pleasure the proposal of holding the new one on the font of baptism being glad to have the opportunity to prove you as well as to the Princess of Weilburg the sincerity of my friendship and feelings."[7] King George was to be the child's godfather and he would be represented by the Earl of Bentinck.[8]

Carolina fell pregnant again in early 1761 and gave birth to a second son, William Louis, on 12 December 1761. The joy of their new family life was shattered just five months later, when their eldest son died at Huis Honselaarsdijk. A devastated Charles Christian wrote to the States-General on 27 May 1762, "It has pleased the Almighty to take my eldest son from this life."[9] Condolences poured in from all over the country as the little Prince was buried with all due honour in the Nassau family crypt in Delft.

The funeral procession left from Huis Honselaarsdijk on 2 June 1762 around 8 o'clock in the evening. In the front walked Court Quartermaster Nieuwerth, accompanied by two attendants carrying torches. They were followed by three carriages behind six horses each and two attendants carrying torches each. The first carriage carried the barons Van der Borg and Van Brandsenburg and counts Schwerin and St. George. The second carriage carried the small coffin underneath a black velvet cloth with silver thread. The last carriage carried Mr De Larrey and De la Potterie. The procession arrived in Delft at 10.30 in the evening, where the little Prince was interred.[10]

Huis Honselaarsdijk did not appear to be a happy place for them. Carolina was not allowed to pick the fruit in the gardens as they were to be sold to others. Charles Christian reportedly quarrelled often with servants and he even caught one stealing. In the memoirs of a steward named Gijsbert Jan van Hardenbroek from that time Carolina is described as, "very rushed and often evil" and she made "the poor Prince so uncomfortable, that he thought it best to take her to their German estates, where he

20

hoped to keep her better under his thumb than when she was with her own family in her own country."[11] It is the most negative report of Carolina's behaviour to be found.

Perhaps in an effort to put the death of their young son behind them, it was decided that they should travel to Weilburg for the first time since their marriage. It was the first time that Carolina and her young brother were be separated for a longer period. He was only just recovering from a serious illness too. This is also the year that the first letters of what would be an extensive correspondence began. Carolina began all her letters to her brother with, "My (very) dear brother" and all the letters speak of a deep attachment between the siblings. Departing from her brother was hard for Carolina and she wrote:

"Be persuaded that my attachment for you would not have allowed me to leave without seeing you if your note had testified to your will and I am very sensitive to your friendship for me. Continue this gracious friendship of which I am delighted. Count always on the tenderness which I bear you and which, if possible, is increased still during the anxieties I have had during your illness. Thus you feel, my dear brother, how sweet it would have been for me to have the consolation of tempting you with the friendliness and tenderness with which I shall be your most devoted servant and your sister, friend, Caroline, Princess of Nassau.

P.S. The Prince charged me to assure you of his respect. He asked the Duke (of Brunswick) to make you his Court; but the Duke did not prefer that and took things on him. My husband commends himself to the continuance of your good graces; I thank you a thousand times for the kiss you have told me to give to Lutz (William Louis) on your behalf. I recommend this little nephew. Take care of yourself and think of me sometimes."[12]

At the time of her departure, William had just turned 15, while Carolina was 20.

Carolina and her husband went to Kirchheimbolanden to a castle that was built around 1602 and which flourished under her husband's renovations. Close by at Oranienstein, a great-aunt of Carolina happened to live. She was Maria Amalia, the sister of Johan William Friso, Prince of Orange, Carolina's grandfather. Her grandmother was delighted that Carolina got to visit family members in the area. But no matter how busy Carolina was, she always managed to find time to write to her brother. "They (these lines) are scribbled, but it comes from a good heart, you know this. We had the Prince and the Princess of Solms lodged here. They came when my aunt Maria was here and we asked them to stay until Monday. These are the best people in this world. [...] Goodbye dear brother love me as I love you."[13] She places special emphasis on "but it comes from a good heart, you know this", by randomly writing it in Dutch.

She gave birth to her first daughter on 5 February 1764 named Augusta Carolina Maria but she soon longed to return to The Hague. But before she could return to The Hague, she sadly wrote to her brother, "At 6 in the morning I had a miscarriage [...] I am well, but I am weak [...] God be praised that my health is good. [...] So you do not worry."[14]

Despite the miscarriage, she still hoped to returned to The Hague in November. "We long to see you again, my dear brother, I hope that I shall have the satisfaction of embracing you in the middle of November."

Meanwhile, Marie Louise had been ill for some time and in early 1765 she had begun to complain about being out of breath more often. She had already had several lights attacks in the last few years. In the middle of March she had attended her last church service, and several people had noticed that she greeted them kindly, as if to say goodbye.[15] She began to prepare for death and hoped to live until Easter so that she could go to church. She was very unwell on the Saturday before Easter, although she did sign several letters. Later that same day, she got a fever and became short of breath. She gave the order that the Easter service was not be disrupted, but by the next Monday it leaked out that she was ill.[16] Around 11 o'clock that evening, she was left unable to speak, except occasionally gasping "Oh, God!" A preacher attempted to comfort her with hymns and passages from the bible. Marie Louise of Hesse-Kassel died on 9 April 1765, with William and Carolina by her side.[17] Of their three guardians appointed at the death of their mother, only the Duke of Brunswick was still alive.

Carolina, her brother and their aunt Amalia's son were their grandmother's heirs and they all received an equal share of the jewels and the gold. Carolina received blue china, while William received the coloured Saxon china. By means of a lottery, Carolina received her grandmother's paintings. Marie Louise was buried in the Grote Kerk in Leeuwarden. Unfortunately, her grave was ransacked in 1795.[18]

Her brother had only just turned 17 and was 11 months away from his 18th birthday. Carolina was 22 and she was three months pregnant with her fourth child. She would fulfil the last few months of William's minority as his regent.

Around this time the building of a palace was begun for the couple at the Korte Voorhout in The Hague. It was not far from Noordeinde Palace and was designed by architect Pieter de Swart, who had been under the patronage of Carolina and William's father. He designed it in a Louis XVI style and it was 77 metres wide and three stories high. When the architect died in 1773, the building was not finished. Currently, only the west wing of the building still stands as part of the original plans of the building. Despite its unfinished state, Carolina held court there and it was a grand mix of artists and musicians, most notably nine-year-old Wolfgang Amadeus Mozart.

William left for the Loo Palace in the spring of 1765 to spend the summer there, but Carolina was forced to remain behind, not in the least because of her advancing pregnancy. She immediately wrote to William how she wished she could follow him to their beloved palace. "I go there 20 times a day in my mind." She even offered him advice where he can play his clarinet to get the best acoustics.[19] At the bottom of that same letter to her brother, her eldest surviving son, William Louis writes in big letters and in Dutch: "I am good (I am a good boy). Bye uncle. Ludwig de Nassau." She continued to write her brother every couple of days from The Hague.

In June 1765, Carolina received a royal visitor from England, her first cousin, Prince Edward, Duke of York and Albany, the second son of Frederick, Prince of Wales. She wrote to her brother that he arrived at five o'clock in the evening and did the honour of visiting her. She called him amiable and wrote in big bold letters the Dutch word for kind (VRIENDELIJK) in between sentences. She also wrote that he looked just like his sister but "she looks better than him" because his hair and eyebrows are practically white.[20] At the time, a possible marriage between the Duke's sister Caroline Matilda and William was being discussed. The marriage came to nothing and Caroline Matilda ended up marrying the mentally ill King Christian VII of Denmark the following year. She and the Duke of York and Albany spent time going to the theatre and the opera and she wrote to her brother that The Hague would be the same old again when the Duke left. They must have gotten along well.

She was still well enough to travel in early June to travel and she was delighted to finally be able to see Amsterdam. She wrote a day by day account of the journey to her brother and mentions seeing the ruins of the castle of the Counts of Egmont and the tomb of a count of Holland in a church that she did not think was very beautiful. She described another church as the most beautiful of the Seven Provinces. She also praised the organ inside the church and the sound of it was "superb." She also visited a few normal houses, which she described as doll houses. Overall, she was "quite content" with the trip.[21]

At the end of July, Caroline complained that she is so big that she was not presentable, by then she was around seven months pregnant.[22] By early August, she called her size "ugly."[23] Her husband was able to visit her brother and upon his return to The Hague Carolina wrote a gushing letter about all the good things her husband told her. "Among other things, you have the best face in the world and that you are charming." In big bold Dutch letters she wrote, "because you are a good man."[24] She missed her brother so much that she compares The Hague to the Sinai Peninsula.

On 28 September 1765 in The Hague, Carolina gave birth to her fourth child, a daughter named Wilhelmine Luise.

Carolina was not only a great lover of music and opera, she was also an accomplished musician. She was taught by Giovanni Battista Zingoni, a tenor who had also worked with Johann Christian Bach. He recognized her natural talent and with his help and the aid of a piano teacher named Jean Bouthmy, she became an accomplished pianist.[25]

Wolfgang Amadeus Mozart was born on 27 January 1756 and he had shown prodigious abilities from his early childhood. Carolina first became acquainted with him on 12 September 1765 when the nine-year-old Mozart visited The Netherlands as part of his travels. He and his family had been making various European trips from 1762. Mozart's father wrote, "On the very day of our departure the Dutch envoy drove to our lodgings and discovered we had gone to Canterbury for the races, after which we would be leaving England. He was in a trice and begged me to go to The Hague, saying that the Princess of Weilburg – the sister of the Prince of Orange – was extraordinarily anxious to see this child about whom she had heard and read so much. In a word, he and everyone else had so much to say on the subject, and the proposal was so attractive that I had to decide to come, not least because, as you know, one shouldn't refuse a pregnant woman."[26]

He travelled with his parents and his sister, who was also a gifted musician. The journey was often difficult and the children suffered under the poor conditions. Mozart had fallen ill before arriving in The Hague and his sister fell ill shortly after arrival. Young Mozart performed his initial concert before Carolina alone after his sister developed a severe cold. Her cold turned into typhoid fever and she was given the last sacrament on 21 October. Carolina sent her own physician, professor Schwenke to care for the fourteen-year-old girl. Whatever he did, it worked and a few days later she was able to get up again.[27]

Mozart was driven to Caroline's palace at the Korte Voorhout in The Hague in a carriage specifically designed for him. He also played for Carolina's brother and a public concert took place on 30 September, where father and son both played solos. They were joined by musicians from the court orchestra and orchestras from the city. While Mozart's sister was on the mend, Mozart himself fell ill around 15 November 1765, he possibly also had typhoid. His father wrote, "He is absolutely unrecognisable, nothing more than delicate skin and small legs." He was given a enema on the 23rd and was dangerously ill on the 30th. He was a little better by the 1st of December but he went eight days without speaking. His tongue was dry "like wood" and the skin on his lips was hard and black.[28] Professor Schwenke was again sent to the rescue. At the beginning of January 1766, the entire family was well enough to perform together. On 22 January 1766, they organized a public concert and father, son and daughter all performed. After this concert, the family moved on to Amsterdam.

As the Netherlands prepared a feast for the coming-of-age of William, Mozart composed eight variations of the aria, "Laat ons juichen, Batavieren!" (Let us cheer, Batavians!) on the orders of Carolina. They were done just in time for William's birthday and were even announced in the newspapers. Carolina was known to often sing "her" aria. After his illness, Mozart also composed six sonnets for her, which were released later in 1766 as Opus 4, with the title *"Six sonates pour le clavecin avec l'accompagnement d'un violon dédiés à Madame la Princesse Nassau-Weilburg, née Princesse d'Orange, Par W. Mozart agé de 9 ans."*[29] These sonnets are written for both the piano and the violin and they were most likely premiered at the birthday celebrations for William by Mozart and his father. The sonnets were not published until 16 April and at the time they cost three guilders. Mozart also played several variations of the Dutch national song for his guests.[30]

Accompanying the six sonnets was a letter from Mozart. "To your Highness, the Princess of Nassau-Weilburg, etc,

– Madame

On the point of leaving Holland, I can not think of this moment without pain. The virtues of her Highness, her greatness, her goodness, which has brought me back to life, the gentleness of her voice, the pleasure of accompanying her, the honour of paying tribute to them with my feeble talents and my sensitive heart will be there forever. Have they, Madame, the mercy to receive a proof of this? You will be glad to hear this fear of my night, and have the mercy to look at it as a sign of my sincere gratitude and the deep respect with which I am, madame, Your Highness, the most high, the most subordinate, the most obedient, the smallest servant. J.G. Wolfgang Mozart from Salzburg."[31]

The birthday celebrations for William lasted from 7 March until 12 March. It was described as a "miracle of light", which no one had ever seen before.[32] At the end of March, the Mozart family left The Hague, but Carolina's "smallest servant" would be back 12 years later.

Suddenly there are no more letters in the Royal Archives from Carolina until 1769. She gave birth to a stillborn and nameless daughter on 21 October 1767.[33] Another son was born on 25 October 1768, he was named Frederick William. The year 1767 was also the year that her brother married Wilhelmina of Prussia, a daughter of Prince Augustus William of Prussia and Luise of Brunswick-Wolfenbüttel. They had married in Berlin and now lived in The Hague. It was time to let her brother go and move on. Charles Christian was itching to go back to his own lands.

Portrait of Anne, Princess Royal and Princess of Orange (1753),
attributed to Johann Valentin Tischbein

**Portrait of William IV, Prince of Orange (1751),
attributed to Johann Valentin Tischbein**

**Portrait of King George II of Great Britain (1744),
attributed to Thomas Hudson**

Portrait of Carolina of Orange-Nassau as a child (1743 - 1755)
attributed to Robert Mussard

Portrait of William IV with wife and daughter in Amsterdam in 1747
(1853 - 1861)

Portrait of Carolina of Orange-Nassau as a child (1743 - 1755)
attributed to Robert Mussard

Portrait of Anne, Princess Royal and Princess of Orange with her son
William V, Prince of Orange and her daughter Carolina of Orange-
Nassau (1751 - 1803), attributed to Christian Friedrich Fritzsch

Portrait of William V, Prince of Orange (circa 1768-1769), attributed to Johann Georg Ziesenis

Death of Anne, Princess Royal with William and Carolina in mourning (1780 - 1795), after Jacobus Buys

Marriage of Carolina and Charles Christian (1760)

Baptism of Carolina's first son (1761)

Portrait of Carolina with her children (1775), attributed to Anton Wilhelm Tischbein

Portrait of Carolina of Orange-Nassau (1735 - 1807), attributed to
Hendrik Pothoven after Pieter Frederik de la Croix

Portrait of Carolina of Orange-Nassau (1757), attributed to Tethart
Philipp Christian Haag after Jean-Etienne Liotard

Chapter 3

Life as the Princess of Nassau-Weilburg

As she began to set up her court in Kirchheimbolanden, she also began to set up a small orchestra. German composer and poet Christian Friedrich Daniel Schubart wrote of Carolina, "The reigning Princess of this house has earned a great reputation as a connoisseur and protector of music and she sang excellently but on physical grounds, she let the songs go and devoted herself entirely to the piano. From Schobert, Bach, Vogler and Becker, with great ease."

We don't know when Schubart wrote this account of Carolina. The "physical grounds" he speaks of may have been yet another pregnancy that hindered her singing.[1] The composer Carl Ditters von Dittersdorf also described seeing Carolina play the piano. "In these concerts, during which I have appeared every time, I listened to the Princess Frederica (Frederica Charlotte of Prussia, later Duchess of York and Albany as the wife of Prince Frederick, Duke of York and Albany, a son of King George III and Charlotte of Mecklenburg-Strelitz), as well as the Princess of Orange on the forte piano. The latter can do more than could be expected of such high persons." Reportedly, these concerts took place in Berlin but Carolina does not mention them in the letters to her brother.[2] She did mention dabbling in composing a bit herself and in 1769 she asked her brother if he liked the march she has composed.[3]

Caroline found kindred spirits in a small theatre in Kirchheimbolanden and she often wrote of performances at that theatre. Sometimes the actors came to the castle to perform.[4] She did not like sad music and the musicians at her court adapted themselves to their mistress's tastes. They created music in bright and friendly tones.[5] Schubart did criticize the orchestra that Carolina had put together. "With the exception of the concertmaster (named Rothfisher), the members of the orchestra are not very brilliant. They are more accustomed to musical harmony."[6] Carolina's husband might have been the one to pay for all these musical enterprises, but he let Carolina take complete control. She even closed the contract with the concertmaster herself. She even had a musician named Hartenberg, who played the harp for her every day and Mozart himself estimated that she had around 300 musicians in her service in 1778.[7]

Charles Christian was eager to develop his own lands. He began improvements in education, by introducing new schoolbooks and he combatted poverty by supporting orphans and widows. He was also for religious freedom and even went as far as protecting Roman Catholic funeral rites with a military force. It led to a rebellion that had to be put down by 800 men sent by the Elector Palatine.[8] It soon became clear that the annual visits to Weilburg were not enough to rule it and in 1769 Charles Christian decided to live permanently in Weilburg. He and his growing family moved to Weilburg and in May 1769 the letters between Carolina and William start up again. "My dear brother, I wanted to be discrete and not write to you, but I could not resist." William too was eager to write to her and she received a letter from him, before her own had even been delivered to him. "I was delighted to receive your dear letter, and see that you thought of me before you even received my letter."[9] Carolina had grown fond of William's wife and often mentioned her in her letters as "Madame la Princesse." William and Wilhelmina had suffered the loss of a son, who had only lived for a day in March. Carolina also inquired after two black servants that William had hired. "Excuse my curiosity, how are Cidron and Cupidon, or the little devils, doing?"[10] Carolina continued to follow the Dutch news and she read newspapers from The Hague.[11]

By late June 1769, Carolina talked about cherries and strawberries that she couldn't stop eating. They were small but delicious and she offered to send her brother some so that he could grow them at the Loo Palace.[12] It may have been early pregnancy cravings. She also mentioned how her four children could not stop talking about their uncle, which may have been slightly enthusiastic as the youngest wasn't even a year old yet. She confirmed her pregnancy in early August. "I find myself pregnant again and expect to give birth towards the beginning of February."[13] In the same letter she wished Wilhelmina a happy birthday, she had just celebrated her 18th birthday. William wrote back to congratulate her on her pregnancy and Carolina excitedly wrote back that perhaps her eldest son could write to him soon without her assistance.[14] And so little Louis did on 17 September 1769. In big bold French letters, he wrote to his uncle, "My dear uncle, Mother told me you wanted a letter from me. I am writing this one to ask how you are doing. My respects to my aunt and my sisters presents you theirs."[15] Just three months later, the young boy wrote to his uncle for a second time. "I thank you for my sisters, my brother, and for the beautiful presents you have had the goodness to send us."[16]

In August, Carolina attended a ball with her young daughters Maria and Luise. Young Luise danced with the person throwing the ball and Carolina described laughing like a little girl. "My children are growing up", she wrote to her brother in November 1769.[17] Carolina was a little depressed around the new year as she wrote to her brother, "Your old sister ("Oude sus was written in Dutch, while the rest is in French) embraces you with all her heart. Do continue your precious friendship, which is one of the sweetest things in my life."[18] She was feeling better by her next letter and quipped the Dutch proverb, "Oncruit vergaat niet" or "weeds do not perish so easily." She was by then nearing the end of her pregnancy, but her due date came and went. Just days before giving birth, she continued to write to her brother about the death of Charles Yorke, Lord Chancellor of Great Britain on 20 January 1770. She even requested that he sent her his exact measurements so that she could embroider a jacket for him. Surprisingly, the request was written in English, rather than in French or Dutch.

She gave birth to a daughter named Carolina Louise Friederike on 14 February 1770 and was back to writing letters two weeks later, on her own birthday, although the letter is rather short for Carolina. She thanks her brother for his congratulations on her birthday and that of the birth of "my Carolina."[19] She was in "excellent health" and as Lent approached she jokingly added an anecdote from their youth when William got indigestion from eating too many pancakes. She had been churched by the middle of March and was back enjoying her social life.[20] Her children were well and "Fritz" (her second surviving son) was getting taller and loved his sisters.[21]

Around this time, Charles Christian left for The Hague for military duties and this time Carolina was left behind with the children. Carolina was not happy about being left behind. "Why can he not put me in a pocket?" she wrote sadly to her brother.[22] If she was sad about her husband's departure, she would be struck by an even greater tragedy all by herself. Her eldest surviving son, William Louis, died suddenly after a short time in his sickbed on 16 April 1770. That same day she wrote, "The friendship which we have had for each other in our childhood leaves me no doubt as to the part you will take in the sensible loss which we have just made by the death of my dear Louis, who died this morning at five o'clock after a 7-day illness. Farewell, love me always, it will serve as a consolation to this afflicted heart which since your life began has cherished and loved you."[23] William quickly allowed for Charles Christian to return to his wife to mourn the death of their son and gave their sole surviving son Frederick, who was not even two-years-old at the time, the military honours that his elder brother had held.

"I am extremely sensible of the part you have taken in the grief which my dear Louis has caused me, and I can not find words strong enough to thank you for having allowed the Prince to come and join me and to show you my gratitude for your goodness. I weep for what you have done for my Frederick by granting him what his brother had. I hope that Fritz will merit what you have done for him.

Farewell, the best of brothers. I hope that God will grant my wishes for you and for the Princess so that he may preserve you from all that might be unpleasant to you. The Prince who arrived yesterday evening presents his respects to you."[24]

Just two weeks later she wrote, "God has given me the grace of not abandoning me, and has, therefore, in this misfortune more firmness than I should have dared to hope. The Prince regretted infinitely that he had not been able to remain until the end of the exercises."[25]

Charles Christian wanted his wife to visit the Landgravine of Hesse-Kassel at the Castle of Philippsruhe in Hanau, whose company she enjoyed and might distract her somewhat. The Landgravine was born Princess Mary of Great Britain and she was a daughter of George II of Great Britain and Caroline of Ansbach. She was a younger sister of Carolina's mother Anne. Carolina described her as "the best of women, as well as our worthy and adorable mother." Carolina set off for Hanau at the beginning of May. Nevertheless, Carolina found it hard to forget her son. "I cannot dispel my sadness, which pursues me everywhere. The image of my Lutz is always present and I miss it all the time. I was ungrateful and I was insensible to all the goodnesses. I flatter myself that God has made me subject to his will."[26] She tried to focus on her surviving children, six-year-old Marie, four-year-old Luise, one-year-old Frederick and two-month-old Carolina. "Carolina is a brunette and experts say she resembles her father. Marie has grown a lot and is becoming wise. Luise also grew up and against my expectation has become lively, she was so quiet once. Fritz, who is fat and pretty, speaks a little, saying Daddy, mama, yes and no. Thus no idle word has yet emerged from his mouth. He looks like my dear Lutz, whose memory still causes me sad moments." She didn't stay in Hanau for very long and was back home in Kirchheimbolanden in the middle of June.

She received a joyous message from The Hague in November of 1770. Wilhelmina had given birth to a child who had lived. It was a daughter who was named Frederica Louise Wilhelmina. She would go by the name Louise. William requested that his beloved sister would stand as godmother to his daughter. There was no question that Carolina would say no. "I joyfully accept the honour you have given me of naming me a godmother to my niece. I embrace my goddaughter with all my heart. Goodbye, papa, my very dear Compère."

On the day of Princess Louise's baptism, Carolina toasted Louise's health with a "kandeel", a warm drink made of milk or wine with egg yolks, sugar and cinnamon. She was probably represented by a proxy at Louise's baptism, as was the norm. The birth of Louise marked a return to her normal self. Carolina began to enjoy music again and she visited the opera in Mannheim. From Mannheim she wrote to William, "The Electoral Palace is very large and beautiful and the pavement is very good. If ever we have the satisfaction of seeing you here in the summer, I would suggest that we take you there when the court is there. For you who loves plays, you will enjoy it royally. But I can already hear you say, my sister is on her talking chair (praatstoel) and her verbiage is long and you would be right!"[27]

In the spring of 1771, Charles Christian returned to The Hague to a large exercise with his regiment. However, this time William insisted that Carolina and the children came with him, as he had not seen them for so long. "I can not express the contentment which I feel of, even before long, paying court to the Princess and embracing you and the dear Louise. I am, as well as the Prince, very sensitive to the goodness which you have for our children, by showing the desire to see them. But as the prince has a great deal of business on his hands, which will render his stay extremely short, and besides, the journey is long and tiring for them, if it is hot, it is hardly possible for us to take them. The only idea of seeing my dear brother, his wife and his little one filled me with joy and satisfaction." Carolina returned to the Loo Palace alone. She was glad to see her sister-in-law and her little goddaughter Louise or Loulou.[28]

During this time, the Danish court was in turmoil as Caroline Matilda of Great Britain, once thought of as a bride for William but who later married King Christian VII of Denmark, was exiled from the court for an extramarital affair with the King's physician, Johann Friedrich Struensee. It was widely assumed that her daughter was in fact the natural daughter of Struensee. "The revolution in Denmark is terrible. I can say that I was surprised. Struensee looks good without a head. God be blessed that you have another wife than that Queen (This sentence was written in English rather than in French). I give thanks to heaven."[29] Caroline Matilda was later exiled to Celle in Germany, where she died in 1775 of scarlet fever at the age of 25.

In August 1771 Carolina was sad to learn of Wilhelmina's miscarriage. She could certainly relate with her sister-in-law. "I take this accident which must have worried you a lot but you see in me the evidence that one can produce children."[30] She would experience almost the same thing just under a year later. She gave birth to a son named Charles Ludwig on 19 July 1772, but he died just eight days later on 27 July. "I send the pen to the Prince to thank you with all my heart, on the part you have read, to take the lively and short joy which was my happy deliverance and the birth of Charles. My health has not suffered by the sorrow of the loss of this dear child."[31] Although she appears to have recovered from the birth normally, she did say, "My health is not quite good, but I am not sick but I am what the Dutch would call a little bit talmpot (*lamenting or whining*)."[32]

Her spirits were lifted somewhat with the happy delivery

of her nephew, who would become King William I of the Netherlands long after her death. She was once again asked to be godmother and she accepted the honour. She even gave the little boy the nickname she had given her own brother once. "I accept with much satisfaction the title of godmother of which you do me the honour of giving me. I embrace my two godchildren often in thought ... I am curious to know if Loulou will call her brother Bololo and if the little chap will patiently endure it as his father did."[33]

In 1772, Carolina's husband received yet another honour from her brother, he was named Governor of Maastricht, a city in the south of the Netherlands. Carolina was overjoyed at the opportunity as this would also allow her to see her brother and his family more often. "I can not express how much I appreciate the goodness you have had in disposing of the government of Maastricht in favour of the Prince. Receive my tender and sincere thanks, as well as for all that you write to me, obliging for us on this occasion. Be persuaded, my dear brother, that my recognition is unbounded and that what makes it most enjoyable is the hope that it gives me to see you more often."[34]

While in Maastricht, they probably lived in the Oude Gouvernement, which Charles Christian had renovated and was the residence of the Governor of Maastricht. If she expected her brother's family to visit often, she was mistaken. It would take until 1776 for her to receive a visit from her brother, his wife and daughter Louise.

There is again a gap in the letters by Carolina stored in the Royal Archives from December 1772 until June 1776. There are a few letters from Charles Christian, one of which is from 23 February 1774 and he congratulated William and Wilhelmina on the birth of their second son, Frederick. He also wrote that he expected his wife to return in March with their children, so she must have returned to their lands in Germany during that time. On 1 May 1775, Carolina gave birth to their second surviving son Charles Frederick William. Charles Christian mentions his son's baptism and his godparents, the Margravine of Baden (Carolina Louise of Hesse-Darmstadt), Ferdinand, Prince of Solms-Braunfels and Prince Frederick of Nassau-Usingen (later Duke of Nassau). He also quipped that his son already had a good appetite. Just four days after the birth, he wrote that his wife was doing well and sent him her compliments. On 8 May, he wrote to William that "le petit Charles" is doing well, thanks be to God.[35] During those years, she and Charles Christian lived alternately in Maastricht, Weilburg or Kirchheimbolanden.

By the time Carolina's letters begin again, she is pregnant again. She gave birth to a daughter named Amalie Charlotte on 6 August 1776 in Kirchheim. Charles Christian writes to William that same night, "My wife has just given birth this morning to a girl. The mother and child (who bears the names of Amalie Charlotte Wilhelmina Louise) are grateful to God, and I have every reason to hope for a speedy recovery."[36]

When Mozart returned to Carolina's court in 1778, she was settled in Kirchheimbolanden. He must have remembered how she sent her own physician to save his life and that of his sister and the sonnets he wrote for her. For Carolina, having Mozart come to her musical court was a crowning moment.

She greeted him with, "Yes, dear Mozart, who have you brought with you?" He introduced his companion, "The most noble princess, Your Highness, I beg your pardon. Because I know, from Holland, how you loves to sing your gospel. I have brought with me a very special young singer from Mannheim, Mademoiselle Aloysia Weber." Carolina welcomed Mademoiselle Weber, "I am sure, dear Mozart, that it is right for me. Welcome, Mademoiselle Weber and Monsieur Weber! (The singer was just 15-years-old and was escorted by her father). But, Monsieur Mozart, describe to me what happened after 1766. Many of my guests are also interested, because I often told them about that time!"[37]

On Sunday 25 January 1778, Mozart and the Webers went down to the Catholic Church, where he played the grand organ. On Monday, Mozart played the Dutch national song and several variations he composed in 1765 for a few of Carolina's guests. Carolina also played for her guests and she sang an aria. A day later, Carolina again played for her famous guest, this time she surprised him with work with the Frenchman Schober. Reportedly, the applause was neverending. She did it for Mozart's 22nd birthday, which he had not expected. Where he came from, name days were considered to be more important than birthdays. He was left amazed by Carolina's outpouring of love. Later that night, Carolina played the piano, while Mozart asked for a violin. The concert lasted for over two hours.[38]

On Wednesday, Aloysia and Mozart entertained at the palace for the last time. They had already been gifted food for the return journey by Carolina, including deer shot by her husband during his last hunt. "Dear Mozart, because he once again enjoyed me with his charming music and gave me four symphonies, he was to receive seven Louis d'or (coins with the image of King Louis XIII, the actual value fluctuated) from me. The Mademoiselle Weber, who is quite a talented singer, she is to receive five Louis d'or. I think that this is a good payment. I wish them, Monsieur Mozart and Mademoiselle Weber a happy future. God bless you!"

Mozart and the Webers departed on 29 January 1778 and headed towards Worms.[39]

In 1778, Carolina and her children were painted by Anton Wilhelm Tischbein. She looked healthy and young in the painting. She was wearing a bright blue gown and her daughters were wearing similarly bright colours, while her sons were wearing darker colours. She wrote to her brother that she kept the painting a secret for her husband as a surprise and "the resemblances are all fairly good, although they can not all be perfectly alike."[40] In that same letter, she compared her many pregnancies to those of Charlotte of Mecklenburg-Strelitz, Queen of Great Britain and Ireland, as the wife of George III, who had fifteen children. In the middle of the letter she switched from French to Dutch, describing herself to be "in a blessed state" and "my dear brother, I shall be glad if it is a well-made Prince and even if it is a beautiful Princess I will be pleased when I hold it. Do I not write beautifully in our mother tongue?" Tragically, the child she was expecting was indeed a beautiful Princess, but the little girl was stillborn on 21 October 1778. Charles Christian wrote to his brother-in-law, "I have the honour to inform Your Highness that my wife was delivered on the 21st of this month at 3 o'clock in the morning, although it was not a happy delivery, as the girl was born dead. She is doing as well as one might desire at the present."[41] The very next year, she again suffered the loss of a stillborn child, but there is no mention of the child in her letters or in those of her husband, so we do not know if it was a boy or a girl.[42]

In April 1779, ten-year-old Prince Frederick joined his father in the army and was separated from his mother for the first time. "I know they cannot constantly be by my side, but the moment of separation was very difficult for me", she wrote to her brother.[43] During the winter, the family was hit by an outbreak of smallpox. Despite the birth of the stillborn child sometime in 1779, she fell pregnant again around September and was several months pregnant when the smallpox hit. She was worried about her children, but her pregnancy appeared to be going well. "I happily advance in my pregnancy, despite the sorrow that the sickness of my children has caused me. Luise is no better yet. You must submit to the will of God, but my heart is often torn. Although you are overwhelmed with affairs which for the most part are unpleasant, you still find time to talk with me."[44] Despite her sorrows, she also remembered to congratulate her brother on his 32nd birthday. Luckily, no one in Carolina's family died of the smallpox, which seems lucky for a disease which caused so much death.

The unpleasant affairs Carolina talked about concern the troubles with England, which would turn into the Fourth Anglo-Dutch War later that year.

She gave birth to another beautiful Princess in April 1780. Charles Christian happily wrote to William, "I have nothing more pressing than to announce to Your Highness than that my wife has just happily been delivered of a girl on the 22nd between 10 and 11 o'clock in the evening."[45] The Princess was named Henriette and she lived. It must have been a great relief for Carolina after two stillborn children.

In 1781, Prince Frederick was getting ready to go to the University of Leipzig but William preferred that the boy go to the University of Leiden or Utrecht, which were of the reformed religion. William knew that Frederick could still one day be stadtholder, should his own line die out. In the summer of 1781, Carolina visited The Hague once more, but it was not to be a happy summer. William was being blamed for neglecting the fleet, suppressing freedom of speech and selling the country out to England. Carolina was deeply hurt by the accusations. "Scatter his enemies, confound their knavish tricks [...] God save our poor Republic."[46]

In 1784, Charles Christian was recalled to Maastricht, but he only reluctantly went. He had been busy securing the hereditary rights of Burggravine Louise Isabelle of Kirchberg, who he saw as a suitable bride for his son, Frederick. Louise was the last of Kirchbergs and thus heiress to her father's estates but William simply could not grant Charles Christian leave to return home to sort this all out. Later that year, Charles Christian requested that he and his son be released from Dutch service. William desperately attempted to keep his brother-in-law but it become more and more clear that Charles Christian's future was with his German lands and not with his Dutch brother-in-law. William wrote to Charles Christian in a last ditch attempt to keep him by his side, "I can not decide without Your Highness's advice. I am not crazy enough to want to everything on myself, having seen nothing, being the first general of the world and that I can do all myself."[47] Carolina did not disapprove of her husband's decision but she was very unhappy. "The continuance of your friendship for the Prince and your godson is necessary to my happiness and I would have been unhappy with the idea that my dear Prince's approach might have cooled your sentiments, which are dearer to me than life."[48] She also requested that Frederick's place in the army be transferred to her second son, Prince Charles, then just nine-years-old. Perhaps it was an attempt to please her brother. "He has the most tender and respectful attachment to his uncle and he gratefully acknowledges the favours you have bestowed upon him."[49]

In November 1784, Carolina gave birth to another child, but it died within a few days and we don't know the gender. In March 1785, Carolina celebrated both her silver wedding anniversary and her brother's birthday, which had always been a grand affair where Caroline was concerned. This time they held a gala. "That 5th of March saw a couple unite, which is filled with tenderness and friendship for you."[50] Her children were growing up quickly, Frederick married Burggravine Louise Isabelle of Kirchberg and in the summer of 1785 her daughter Carolina became engaged to the eldest son of the Count of Wied-Runkel and Louise married Henry XIII, Prince Reuss of Greiz. While her children were off starting families of their own, Carolina too was pregnant, but this would be the last time. In November 1785, she again gave birth to a child who died after a few days. This time she found it hard to gather her strength. "My health has not been good for some time. I am better, however I keep to my bed."[51] In cynical Dutch, she added, "I am getting old and cold and I am starting to creak."[52] She was still only 43-years-old at the time, but she had been pregnant 16 times, had given birth to 15 children, of which only seven would live to adulthood. One can only imagine the immense toll this must have taken on her body.

In the autumn of 1786, Carolina wrote with great delight to her brother that she was to become a grandmother and he a great-uncle but early in the next year she wrote, "I hoped that today I could share with you our joy at the birth of a grandson. God has disposed of it and withdrew the child to Him at the time of his birth."[53] Carolina was also sad that Louise did not stay near her but preferred to follow her husband on his many visits to Vienna.

In January 1787, Charles Christian departed for Nijmegen, where the court of the Stadtholder was at the time. He returned the next month and although their meeting had led to nothing, their relationship remained intact, to Carolina's joy. "He assured me that you and the dear ones were doing well, and this assurance always filled me with the most lively joy. Make heaven that my wishes for you are fulfilled in everything and that I can kiss you again before I leave this evil world. I will try to comfort my health so that I can obtain this sweet satisfaction ... my heart cherished you and is all yours. So it was that I heard your first cry and I will take this feeling with me when it pleases God to dispose of me."[54]

Luise and her new husband went to Nijmegen to visit her brother in the spring of 1787. William remembered the visit by sending his sister a silhouette of himself, his wife, their children and Luise and her husband. Carolina was delighted with the present and hung it in her room.[55] "Receive, my dear brother, my tender thanks for the charming gift you gave me. You can not imagine the pleasure it has given me, and I have already spent many moments in contemplation before this charming and precious picture. The resemblances all seem to me to be very near. I have never seen a silhouette of Prince Reuss more striking and as for you, my dear brother, I recognize you still." This letter was dated 13 April 1787.

Her letter dated 27 April 1787 would be the last to her "tres chère frere". She may not have known it at the time, but it sort of reads like a goodbye letter. "I embrace amiable youth tenderly in thought. Farewell, my dear brother. Believe me, for life is all yours."

Carolina died suddenly, after an illness of just two days on 6 May 1787. She was still only 44-years-old. Her heartbroken husband wrote to William, "God has just taken my wife this morning to Him after a sickness of two days. Duty obliges me to communicate it to your Highness; but his good heart will forgive me for not entering into any detail. I lost too much to do it. Mr. de la Pottrie, who will have the honour of handing you this letter, will be able to give you a more just report of the death."[56]

Mentions of her funeral are rare. She was buried in the reformed Peterskirche in Kirchheimbolanden while her husband, who would follow her in death not much later, would be buried in the Lutheran Paulskirche, also in Kirchheimbolanden.[57]

Carolina herself believed that the woman that she had become was entirely due to her admiration for one woman, her mother. We can only admire Anne, the daughter of an English King, whose life had definitely not been easy in the Dutch Republic, to have raised her daughter to be so thoroughly Dutch. She may have written in French, as was common at the time, but her thoughts were Dutch, the language spoken in the family was Dutch and her very first letters were in Dutch.

Chapter 4

Her Legacy and Descendants

In August of 1787, Charles Christian wrote to William to inform him that his daughter Carolina was set to marry the Hereditary Count of Wied-Runkel in two weeks time. It is the last letter by Charles Christian stored in the Royal Archives. Carolina indeed married Karl Ludwig on 4 September 1787, but they would have no children. Charles Christian was reported to have felt a "disturbing solitude" upon his wife's death and he entered into a relationship with a woman named Barbara Giessen and although he denied it, there were rumours of a marriage. The Genealogisches Staatshandbuch, published in 1835, states that Charles Christian married Barbara, the daughter of a barrister, in November 1788 but that information may be incorrect. Charles Christian had an accident on 25 November 1788 and he died of a stroke on 28 November 1788.[1]

Not all of Carolina and Charles Christian's children went on to have offspring. Their eldest daughter Maria became a nun at Quedlinburg and Herford. Luise, whose first son tragically died on the day he was born, went on to have two more sons who lived. Frederick and Isabelle Louise went on to have four children, although one died in infancy. Their second son Charles remained unmarried and had no issue. Amalie Charlotte married Victor II, Prince of Anhalt-Bernburg-Schaumburg-Hoym and they had four children. Their last surviving child Henriette went on to marry Duke Louis of Württemberg and they had five children. Some of their children kept in touch with their uncle, even after their parents had died and some of those letters are in the Royal Archives.

Carolina and Charles Christian's descendants sit on the thrones of Luxembourg, the Netherlands, Belgium, Denmark,

Norway, Sweden, the United Kingdom and Spain.

Luxembourg

Princess Carolina of Orange-Nassau
Frederick William, Prince of Nassau-Weilburg
William, Duke of Nassau
Adolphe, Grand Duke of Luxembourg
William IV, Grand Duke of Luxembourg
Charlotte, Grand Duchess of Luxembourg
Jean, Grand Duke of Luxembourg
Henri, Grand Duke of Luxembourg

Netherlands

Princess Carolina of Orange-Nassau
Frederick William, Prince of Nassau-Weilburg
William, Duke of Nassau
Helena of Nassau
Emma of Waldeck and Pyrmont
Wilhelmina of the Netherlands
Juliana of the Netherlands
Beatrix of the Netherlands
King Willem-Alexander of the Netherlands

Belgium

Princess Carolina of Orange-Nassau
Frederick William, Prince of Nassau-Weilburg
William, Duke of Nassau
Sophia of Nassau
Carl, Duke of Västergötland
Astrid of Sweden
Albert II of Belgium
King Philippe of Belgium

Denmark
Princess Carolina of Orange-Nassau
Frederick William, Prince of Nassau-Weilburg
William, Duke of Nassau
Sophia of Nassau
Gustav V of Sweden
Gustaf VI Adolf of Sweden
Ingrid of Sweden
Queen Margrethe II of Denmark

Norway
Princess Carolina of Orange-Nassau
Frederick William, Prince of Nassau-Weilburg
William, Duke of Nassau
Sophia of Nassau
Carl, Duke of Västergötland
Martha of Sweden
King Harald V of Norway

Sweden
Princess Carolina of Orange-Nassau
Frederick William, Prince of Nassau-Weilburg
William, Duke of Nassau
Sophia of Nassau
Gustav V of Sweden
Gustaf VI Adolf of Sweden
Gustaf Adolf, Duke of Vasterbotten
King Carl XVI Gustaf of Sweden

United Kingdom
Princess Carolina of Orange-Nassau
Henriette of Nassau-Weilburg
Alexander of Württemberg
Francis, Duke of Teck

Mary of Teck
George VI
Queen Elizabeth II of the United Kingdom

Spain
Princess Carolina of Orange-Nassau
Henriette of Nassau-Weilburg
Amalie of Württemberg
Alexandra of Saxe-Altenburg
Olga Constantinova of Russia
Constantine I of Greece
Paul of Greece
Sophia of Greece and Denmark
King Felipe VI of Spain

Carolina is also the ancestress of the pretenders to two Sicilian thrones, the Saxon throne, the Hanoverian throne and the Bavarian throne.

Two Sicilies
Princess Carolina of Orange-Nassau
Frederick William, Prince of Nassau-Weilburg
Henrietta of Nassau
Maria Theresa of Austria
Alfonso, Count of Caserta
Carlos of Bourbon-Two Sicilies
Alfonso, Duke of Calabria
Carlos, Duke of Calabria
Pedro, Duke of Calabria

or
Princess Carolina of Orange-Nassau
Frederick William, Prince of Nassau-Weilburg
Henrietta of Nassau

Maria Theresa of Austria
Alfonso, Count of Caserta
Ranieri, Duke of Castro
Ferdinand, Duke of Castro
Carlo, Duke of Castro

(disputed succession)

Saxony
Princess Carolina of Orange-Nassau
Henriette of Nassau-Weilburg
Maria Dorothea of Württemberg
Joseph Karl of Austria
Margrethe Klementine of Austria
Elisabeth Helene of Turn und Taxis
Anna of Saxony
Alexander of Saxe-Gessaphe

or

Princess Carolina of Orange-Nassau
Frederick William, Prince of Nassau-Weilburg
William, Duke of Nassau
Adolphe, Grand Duke of Luxembourg
William IV, Grand of Luxembourg
Sophie of Luxembourg
Prince Timo of Saxony
Prince Rudiger of Saxony

(Disputed succession)

Hanover
Princess Carolina of Orange-Nassau
Henriette of Nassau-Weilburg

Amelia of Württemberg
Marie of Saxe-Altenburg
Ernest Augustus, Crown Prince of Hanover,
Ernest Augustus, Duke of Brunswick
Ernest Augustus, Prince of Hanover
Ernst August, Prince of Hanover

Bavaria
Princess Carolina of Orange-Nassau
Henriette of Nassau-Weilburg
Maria Dorothea of Württemberg
Elisabeth Franziska of Austria
Maria Theresa of Austria-Este
Rupprecht, Crown Prince of Bavaria
Albrecht, Duke of Bavaria
Franz, Duke of Bavaria

Through her aunt, Amalia of Nassau-Dietz, Carolina was also related to the reigning Prince of Liechtenstein. When Joseph Wenzel, the son of the Hereditary Prince of Liechtenstein eventually succeeds as reigning Prince of Liechtenstein, she will also be the ancestress of the reigning Prince of Liechtenstein as his mother, Princess Sophie of Bavaria is a granddaughter of Albrecht, Duke of Bavaria.

Liechtenstein
Princess Carolina of Orange-Nassau
Henriette of Nassau-Weilburg
Maria Dorothea of Württemberg
Elisabeth Franziska of Austria
Maria Theresa of Austria-Este
Rupprecht, Crown Prince of Bavaria
Albrecht, Duke of Bavaria
Max, Duke of Bavaria,

Sophie of Bavaria
Joseph Wenzel of Liechtenstein

Carolina never lived to see her dear brother exiled. The outbreak of the Fourth Anglo-Dutch war in 1780 was the beginning of the end. The Dutch fleet knew it could not beat the English and tried to avoid confrontation. Several overseas trading posts were taken, and some merchant ships too. Against William's will, the states-general made a treaty with the French. The Treaty of Paris in 1783 only confirmed that the Dutch Republic was nothing any more on the international stage.[2] For William, things went from bad to worse. His apparent lack of leadership and his early dependency on the Duke of Brunswick were thrown in his face. William froze up and became more and more isolated. When more of his prerogatives were taken from him, William left The Hague in protest. Wilhelmina and their children left for Leeuwarden. Wilhelmina used the trip to gather supporters and she was shocked to find that William had left The Hague. In September 1786, they moved their court to the Valkhof in Nijmegen, which was easier to defend if necessary.[3] Wilhelmina, sick of her husband's inability to decide, decided to travel to The Hague on her own. It led to one of the most famous scenes in Dutch history, the Princess was arrested near Goejanverwellesluis and taken to a farmhouse, where she was held for several hours. She wrote several letters from there in the middle of the night and was made to return to Nijmegen.[4] Wilhelmina's brother, King Frederick William II of Prussia, considered this a grave insult and in September 1787 Prussian troops crossed the border. The princely family temporarily returned to The Hague, where they were welcomed by crowds.[5]

Wilhelmina had begun to fear for the future of the Dutch Republic when the French Revolution broke out. When King Louis XVI of France was guillotined on 21 January 1793 and the French Republic declared war on the Dutch Republic, her fears were beginning to be realised. The exiled patriots from before attacked and invaded. On 9 October 1794, just the Maas and Rijn rivers separated the Dutch Republic from the French troops. The family had originally planned to travel from Den Helder to northern Germany and then to Brunswick, but this was no longer an option. In all haste, several fishing boats were commandeered in Scheveningen and on 18 January the first boat with Wilhelmina, her daughter-in-law Wilhelmina and grandson William, the future King William II, departed for England. Later that afternoon, William and his son also departed.[6] In England, the family first lived at Kew and later at Hampton Court.

The stadtholdership was officially abolished on 23 February 1795.In Wilhelmina's letters to her daughter Louise, she repeatedly says that William never abdicated but had only temporarily left the country with the permission of the states-general.[7] William himself wrote shortly after arriving in England, "If I will ever see my fatherland again, I do not know but I will never stop loving it, no matter what happens."[8] Prince William V died at his daughter's palace in Brunswick in 1806. His eldest son triumphantly returned to the Netherlands in 1813 to become its first King in 1815. One can only imagine, with the love Carolina had continue to hold for her brother and their country, how proud she must have felt, had she been alive to see it.

Carolina's line returned to the Dutch royal Family when her great-great-granddaughter Emma of Waldeck and Pyrmont married King William III of the Netherlands as his second wife. They had one daughter together, the future Queen Wilhelmina of the Netherlands. He had first been married to Sophie of Württemberg, but all three of their sons would be predecease him.

Yet, despite her strong links to the current royal houses of Europe and the fact that for a while, she was the only hope of the House of Orange-Nassau, Carolina has been mostly forgotten. This may be due to the fact that she died relatively young and was never involved in the events that led to her brother being exiled to England. Nevertheless, she has left her mark on the world, we may never have seen Mozart reach his full potential if he had died of typhoid while visiting The Hague and her many children and grandchildren spread all over Europe. It seems quite sad that she died so young and that she never even got to meet any of her grandchildren. Throughout her life Carolina remained Dutch through and through and if she could have, she probably would've joined the Dutch army herself, instead of her husband.

Carolina and her heirs were still present in the Constitution of 1917 which said, "In the absence of an heir, who is entitled to the Crown according to the four previous articles, this (the crown) will pass to the legitimate male heirs of the sons of the late Princess Carolina of Orange-Nassau, sister of the late Prince William the fifth and spouse of the late Prince of Nassau-Weilburg."[9] In 1922 the constitution was altered to limit the succession to the throne and it no longer mentions Carolina and her heirs. However, as we have seen above, a descendant of hers still sits on the throne today.

Chapter 5

Walking in Carolina's Footsteps

Throughout her life, Carolina and the court she lived in, whether it was the Dutch court or the Nassau-Weilburg court, were always on the move. Some places are still around to visit, some have disappeared over time.

Stadtholderly Court (Stadhouderlijk Hof) in Leeuwarden, the Netherlands
Birth

The Stadtholderly Court in Leeuwarden began its life in 1564/65 when it was built by Boudewijn van Loo. In 1587 the Gedeputeerde Staten of Friesland bought the large house for 12000 guilders for William Louis, Count of Nassau-Dillenburg and Stadtholder of Friesland, Groningen and Drenthe. From this original design, only the basement and the gate remain. It originally consisted of two wings parallel to the street and in 1604 the Gedeputeerde Staten also bought the Dekema House to the west, which became the home of the steward and the secretary. In 1633, it consisted of 37 rooms, hung with over 300 paintings. By 1661 it was being renovated, although it isn't entirely clear what kind of work was being done. In 1664, almost 164 guilders was paid for a new gallery. Early in the 18th century the wedding between Henriette Amalia of Anhalt-Dessau and Henry Casimir II, Prince of Nassau-Dietz led to bigger renovations. Architect Anthonis Coulon, who probably later also led renovations of the Princessecourt, led these renovations. The entire middle facade was replaced, all the windows were replaced and six new rooms were made on the upper floor. The stairs between the middle and eastern wing was replaced with a great stairwell.

Despite its renovations, the court didn't impress everyone.

In 1710, a merchant wrote, "The Stadtholder and Prince lives in a house, which is not very big, with two irregular wings, even private persons have houses like that, if not better ones." The gallery must have been altered also, because by the time of Carolina's parents' marriage it was renovated into a wing with a dance hall, a court chapel, a pharmacy and a bathroom. This part was demolished in 1804. Carolina was born there in 1743. An inventory from 1731 states that the court has 72 rooms and 7 rooms for storage. A visitor would enter through the front house or a corridor with a grand staircase, marble walls and a plastered ceiling, created by Daniël Marot. From here, they would enter a great hall, across from the Garde du Corps hall. In western direction would be the antechamber and the presence chamber, placing them in the middle of the palace. Following the presence chamber were two cabinet rooms. Behind these was the main bedroom, which was still being used by Marie Louise at the time. Two adjacent rooms are called the "dark" room and the small dining room, which were a part of Marie Louise's quarters. This was followed by a dining room for the nobles, which was enclosed by the two wings. On the west side were a long gallery and a small cabinet, while on the east side was another dining room. These rooms were conveniently close to main kitchen and bakery. On the first floor, in the right wing facing the street was Carolina's father's presence chamber, adjacent to his antechamber, bedroom and wardrobe. From the staircase to the west you could enter Marie Louise's antechamber, followed by a presence chamber and two adjacent cabinets. After the cabinets were a large bedroom and a smaller bedroom. The first floor also housed a library with another cabinet, the court master's rooms and a small kitchen. The court master's rooms were later renovated for Carolina. The left wing housed the rooms of Carolina's aunt Amalia. The attic housed the lower servants.[1] Around 62 people would eat daily meals at the Court in 1740.

By 1747 Carolina and her parents had left Leeuwarden for

The Hague.

King William I bought the old Stadtholderly Court in 1814 and it was renamed Royal Palace and it was once again renovated in 1816. During these renovations, the empire windows were put in. Between 1878 and 1881 it stopped being used as a palace and it became the home of the Commissioner of the King, who also changed much about its appearance. In 1971, the county of Leeuwarden had the opportunity to buy the building under the condition that it have a "worthy destination." It was used by the city as a wedding location and it housed city workers and a secretary. It also reverted to using the name Stadtholderly Court again. Since 1996, the building is being used as a hotel and very little remains of the court that Carolina and her parents must have known.[2]

Princessecourt (Princessehof) in Leeuwarden, the Netherlands

Marie Louise of Hesse-Kassel, Carolina's grandmother, purchased this house in 1730, along with a house on the west side to create the complex currently known as the Princessecourt. An L-shaped building has probably stood on the site since around 1540 and some of the foundations remain. Back then it was called the Camminghahuis but it was confiscated in 1580, because the family was Roman Catholic. The newly appointed stadtholder of Friesland, Groningen and Drenthe, William Louis, Count of Nassau-Dillenburg was permitted to live in the Camminghahuis. He only briefly lived there. Wytze van Camminga was awarded the house again in 1602, but he never lived there. His daughter inherited the property and she performed the necessary renovations. In 1650, it was inherited by her daughter Anna Sophia, who offered it for sale in 1662, but a sale was never made. Anna Sophia's heir sold the property to Willem van Haren in 1671 and he purchased the adjacent building as well in 1680. The property fell apart again by 1688, when the western building was inherited by his sister-in-law. The sister-in-law's heir sold the Camminghahuis to Marie Louise in 1730. She moved into the house in 1731, when her son William IV was named stadtholder and began living at the Stadtholderly Court nearby.

The middle part of the property is perhaps the most recognisable today. Its first inhabitant is mentioned in 1643, a certain R. Sixti who died in 1651. An officer named Damas van Loo was the next owner. During his time, the current facade was made. This was sold to Marie Louise for 19000 guilders and she renovated the middle part. The former stables in the east formed the last of the three properties that combined into the Princessecourt.

After Marie Louise's death, the property was sold in three parts. Two parts of the former property now form the Ceramics museum, which has a separate room to celebrate its former famous inhabitant.[3]

Great Church (Grote Kerk) in Leeuwarden, the Netherlands
Baptism

The Great Church in Leeuwarden began its life as a convent church, which was founded in 1245. The convent was closed in 1580 and its library was sold off. When other churches in the city fell into disrepair, the Great Church became its main church. The Nassau family were regular visitors to the church and some were even interred in the crypt. Carolina was baptised there on 10 March 1743 and her grandfather, King George II was a godparent. Her other godparent was her grandmother Marie Louise and it was she who carried the young Princess to the font.

The Great Church still stands today but it has undergone major renovations. The crypt and the remaining part of the convent were restored. The church still holds services and can only be visited as part of a tour.[4]

Oranjewoud, the Netherlands
Summertime

Oranjewoud is first mentioned under the name Schoterwold in the middle of the 16th century. In 1676, three farms were purchased by Albertine Agnes of Nassau, Carolina's great-great-grandmother. She purchased more farms in 1677 and 1678. She enjoyed living there and regularly spent time there.[5] The next owner was her daughter-in-law, Henrietta Amalia of Anhalt-Dessau and she had furniture transferred from Leeuwarden to Oranjewoud in 1689. Plans for a brand new palace began to be realised in 1703. It was built in the popular baroque style. By 1707, the construction was almost done and plans for decoration were made. In 1708, Henrietta Amalia permanently moved in.[6] The building was never completely finished. When Henrietta Amalia died in 1726, her son was already dead, so the property was inherited by her grandson and Carolina's father, William IV. Her widowed daughter-in-law was allowed to use the property at all times.[7]

Carolina, her brother and her mother spent the summer of 1754 in Oranjewoud where they were welcomed by Marie Louise in the middle of June. Anne visited the city of Leeuwarden with Carolina and William on 5 July, where they were welcomed by the mayor and other members of the local government and a guard of honour. They travelled back to Oranjewoud that same day and departed for The Hague in the middle of July.[8]

Oranjewoud was sold in parts in 1813 and the house that currently stands on the site was built in 1829.[9]

The Loo Palace in Apeldoorn, the Netherlands
Youth

The Loo Palace was by far Carolina's favourite place to live and she always longingly mentioned it to her brother. On the ground first stood the "Old" Loo Castle (Loo is an old word for "open place in the woods", which was first mentioned in 1439. In 1684 the future King-Stadtholder William III bought the Old Loo and the surrounding area. The first stone for the "New" Loo was laid in 1685 by his wife and first cousin, the future Queen Mary II. Mary enjoyed walking in the woods there and she had a great interest in the renovations and newly constructed Loo Palace, the main building of which was completed in 1686. A grand design for the gardens was made and eight people worked in the gardens, including an English man named Ralph Mose. Mary died in 1695, without ever seeing her beloved Loo completed. Not much was altered in the appearance of the Loo Palace in Carolina's time but it was emptied out by the Dutch, French and English in the period 1795-1806. King Louis Napoleon choose it as his summer residence and he covered the palace in a white and grey plaster. After the establishment of the Kingdom, the Loo Palace became the summer residence of the royal family. King William III added an art hall to the east wing in 1875, for his own painting collection. Queen Wilhelmina made some alterations and renovations and she wished to restore it to its former glory from the time of the King-Stadtholder.[10]

Queen Wilhelmina died at the Loo Palace in 1962 and she lay in state in the chapel. After a period of restoration, it was opened to the public in 1984. The Old Loo is also still there, but remains private property of the Dutch royal family. You can walk in the gardens during the months of April and May.

The Loo Palace is also the home of two portraits of Carolina.

Binnenhof in The Hague, the Netherlands
Official residence of the stadtholder

The Binnenhof was the residence where Carolina's brother was born, but it was also where both her parents lay in state after their deaths.

It began its life as a hunting ground in 1230 for Count Floris IV. In 1248, his son William II, who had been elected German anti-King in 1247, began to build what would later be known as the Ridderzaal, or Hall of Knights, which still stands in the centre of the Binnenhof. William's son, Floris V, had the Court Chapel built and he spent more and more time in The Hague. The Hague did not remain the main residence for very long, although it did become the basis of government. The States-General permanently settled in The Hague in 1588. The Dutch stadtholders continued building on the Binnenhof, as they wished to be near the centre of power. King-Stadtholder William III was born in the residence as was Carolina's brother William.

When Carolina and her family arrived at the Binnenhof in 1747, she came with seven people in her own household.[11] The rooms she would have inhabited were on the second floor of the complex.

During the years of King Louis Napoleon, the seat of government was moved to Amsterdam and the Binnenhof was left to serve as an army hospital and school. After the accession of Carolina's nephew as King William I, it was once again the seat of government and it remains so to this day.[12]

Huis ten Bosch, the Netherlands
Youth

Huis ten Bosch was built by Amalia of Solms-Braunfels for herself and her husband, Stadtholder Prince Frederick Henry in 1645. She was granted a parcel of land measuring 4,700 metres in length and 37,8 acres "to be transformed in planting and construction for her recreation and exercise so as to befit her pleasure." Pieter Post was chosen to see the project through. The first stone was laid by Elizabeth Stuart, Queen of Bohemia, whom Amalia had served as a lady-in-waiting. It is located in the woods near The Hague and was called the "Sael van Orange" or "Hall of Orange" in that time. The building is focussed on a central hall three stories high with a crowned dome on an octagonal drum. On the east and west sides of this central hall were two stories with apartments. The main entrance facade was made of natural stone. The plans for the central hall were altered with the death of Frederick Henry and Amalia dedicated it to the everlasting memory of her husband.

Huis ten Bosch passed to the descendants of Amalia's eldest daughter Louise Henriette in the form of King Frederick I of Prussia, whose son eventually gave it back to Carolina's father. Carolina's father was invested with the Order of the Garter in the central hall, under the images of Frederick Henry's accomplishments. He also initiated renovations and in 1733 the construction of two new wings began, both with central entrances. The central hall was often used for concerts and we can only assume that Anne and Carolina played music there. Carolina and her brother William's rooms were on the main floor of the east wing. The walls of the east wing were covered by paintings from Anne's own hand. Construction went on from 1733 until 1754 and Carolina's father died before it was finished.

It remains largely in its original setting and still functions as a residence for the King of the Netherlands.[13]

Soestdijk Palace, the Netherlands
Residence of the stadtholder

The Soestdijk Palace that Carolina would have known is a far cry from the imposing building that still stands today.

The land was bought in 1638 by the mayor of Amsterdam, Cornelis de Graeff, where he built a modest house with just two floors and an attic. Upon his death in 1664, the house passed to his second son, Jacob and he sold it to William III of Orange, later the King-Stadtholder in 1674. He began expanding the property immediately after buying it. William and his wife Mary spent some time at Soestdijk in 1682, but after they bought the Loo Palace visits to Soestdijk became a rarity. After William's death the Stadtholdership fell to Johan William Friso of Nassau-Dietz, a descendant of William the Silent's brother John VI, Count of Nassau-Dillenburg, but the anti-Orange party used the confusion around William's death to once again abolish the stadtholdership. Johan William Friso drowned in 1711 and he was succeeded by his posthumous son William IV, who was Carolina's father. Johan William Friso's wife Marie Louise and his son only occasionally used Soestdijk Palace. William IV was restored to the Stadtholdership in 1747. Upon his death in 1751, the stadtholdership fell to his son and Carolina's brother, William V. William stayed at Soestdijk shortly after returning from Berlin for his wedding to Princess Wilhelmina of Prussia. Around 1787 it was described, "The castle is not very big. It is actually only suitable as a hunting lodge and could not hold the entire court. There is a nice, painted hall and it also has wallpaper with a fabric of a number of orange trees, which makes it look rather primitive. The bed and the rest of the furniture do not match. [...] The park is very large and currently has over 300 deer."[14]

The tense political situation made it so that William and Wilhelmina barely visited Soestdijk and they fled to England in 1795. It was again used as a palace by King Louis I of Holland, brother of Emperor Napoleon I of France, and he ordered renovations. Upon the return of William V's son as King William I of the Netherlands, Soestdijk was offered to his son, the future King William II for his actions at the Battle of Waterloo. After King William II's death, his wife, Anna Pavlovna of Russia used the palace as a summer residence. Around that time the two major wings of the palace were added. After her death in 1865, it fell to her second son, Prince Henry who was married to Amalia of Saxe-Weimar-Eisenach. He agreed to having a railway track near Soestdijk Palace, which led to an influx of inhabitants in the area and thus drove up property prices. After Henry's death, the palace fell to his brother, King William III, who preferred to stay at the Loo Palace. His second wife, Emma of Waldeck and Pyrmont often used the palace as a summer residence and under her watch electric light and running water were installed in the palace. The palace fell to Queen Wilhelmina upon her mother's death in 1934 and she did not visit it often either. It was used as a residence by her daughter Juliana and her husband Bernhard, even after Juliana became Queen and she is perhaps the best know resident of the palace. She died at her beloved palace in 2004. It was briefly open to the public and at the moment of writing, it was set to become a hotel, at least partly.[15]

Great Church (Grote Kerk) in The Hague, the Netherlands
Wedding

The Great Church in The Hague has a lot of connections to the Orange-Nassau family, beginning with the baptism of the future Prince William II of Orange in 1626, followed by that of the future Prince William III 25 years later. Carolina's brother was baptised in the church in 1748, followed by his children Louise and the future King William I. Carolina's wedding was the first Orange-Nassau wedding to take place there and we know that she wore a silver wedding dress with silver fringes.[16] The next wedding to take place there was that of Carolina's niece, Louise to Karl Georg August, Hereditary Prince of Brunswick-Wolfenbüttel. Over a century later, Queen Wilhelmina married Prince Henry of Mecklenburg-Schwerin, followed by her daughter Juliana's wedding to Prince Bernhard of Lippe-Biesterfield 36 years later. The last Orange-Nassau wedding to take place there was of Prince Constantijn, brother of King Willem-Alexander and Laurentien Brinkhorst in 2001.

A church has stood on the site since around 1280, then built from wood. Around 1335, people began to speak of a "great church" indicating that it had been replaced with a stone building. The current building arose between 1420 and 1424 with its unique hexagonal tower. A major fire in 1539 destroyed much of the building, but it was rebuilt to its former glory and shape and the building still stands today.[17]

Huis Honselaarsdijk, the Netherlands
Early years of marriage

Whoever founded the castle is not known and the eldest known image of a castle on the site dates from 1609. The castle eventually made its way to the hands of the Princes of Orange through the inheritance of Johanna van Polanen, who married Engelbert I of Nassau. In 1615, it was decided to demolish the old castle and begin construction on a new castle. This probably happened around 1620. The construction was finally finished in 1626. The castle fell to King Frederick I of Prussia after the death of King-Stadtholder William III and in 1754 it was transferred to Carolina's brother and his heirs. Architect David van Stolk was ordered to restore both Huis Honselaarsdijk and Noordeinde Palace. The complete restoration was estimated at F40.780 – while selling it would make F28.600 – and for a while Anne was tempted to sell it. Eventually she decided to tear down both wings, although she would leave part of the right wing, and repair the main building. In 1756 the building was completely repainted on the outside. The garden was worked on in 1757 and over 200 trees were planted and two statues, of Jupiter and Mercury, were brought from Breda. In 1760, it became the summer residence of Carolina and her new husband, Charles Christian. They moved in in September 1760. They furnished it partly with their own furniture. Carolina suffered perhaps her greatest loss at Huis Honselaarsdijk. Her eldest son, George William, died there on 27 May 1762. He was not even two-years-old.[18]

They continued to visit Huis Honselaarsdijk in 1762 and 1763 and visited the poet Willem van der Pot several times. In March 1764 they announced they no longer wished to use Huis Honselaarsdijk. Her brother never lived at Huis Honselaarsdijk, he only used it as a hunting lodge. The house fell into decay during the French occupation and was used a hospital and a prison. It was eventually demolished in 1815 and only some of the outbuildings still stand today.[19]

Castle Kirchheimbolanden in Kirchheimbolanden, Germany
Carolina and Charles Christian's residence

Carolina and Charles Christian's residence in Kirchheimbolanden was Castle Kirchheimbolanden. The site has a long history and there has been a residence on the site since the year 600. Under Charles Christian's father a new building was built between 1738 and 1740. He built a completely new palace in the baroque style. The architect was Guillaume d'Hauberat, who already had Mannheim Castle to his name. The palace was located at the foot of a hill, close to the city centre but still with plenty of space for a garden. It had two pavilions, three wings like a horseshoe and a square in the middle. He made Kirchheimbolanden his summer residence and he was often there, because he loved to hunt.[20]

Simultaneously, the nearby Lutheran Paulskirche was built but it is a rather simple church and lacks the splendour of the baroque palace.

The gardens were modelled after French gardens with its figurative forms and were 80.000m2 large. The castle had its glory days under Charles August and later under his son, Charles Christian, who moved the seat of government to Kirchheimbolanden. Carolina is credited with bringing cultural life to blossom at Kirchheimbolanden. It was through her connections that Mozart visited the palace 1778.

Carolina died at Kirchheimbolanden and her husband in the nearby Münster-Dreisen but due to their difference in religion they were not buried together. Carolina was buried in the nearby reformed Peterskirche, while Charles Christian was buried in the Lutheran Paulskirche.[21]

Her son would be forced to flee from the palace by the French Revolution and the French occupied the palace. It signalled the end of its use as a residence. The middle and left wing were torn down but were restored to its former glory for its current use: a senior residence.[22]

Castle Weilburg in Weilburg, Germany
Carolina and Charles Christian's residence

Castle Weilburg is built on top of a mountain, surrounded on three sides by the river Lahn. The city is first mentioned in 906 and a so-called "castellum" existed there. It fell into the hands of the Count of Nassau in the 12th century and it was he who began building a residence. While the main residence of the House of Nassau-Weilburg was moved to Kirchheimbolanden in 1741, by Charles Christian's father, Charles Augustus, the seat of government remained at Weilburg.

The most important expansion was carried out in 1699 and the castle expanded in all four directions. Over 720 workers and 41 soldiers were employed during the expansions. The construction led to massive woodcutting and in 1734 the use of timber was restricted to prevent more damage to the woods. After this, only minor renovations were made. Several plans from the 18th and the 19th century were never carried out and so it remains in the baroque style.

The exterior has a simple facade with sand-coloured plastered walls and sandstone red facades. The castle church is home to the fürstengruft, where several Nassau rulers are buried.

In 1890 the castle passed into Luxembourg's hands and in 1935 it was sold to the Prussian State. As its legal successor, the current owner is the state of Hesse. Parts of it are now a museum and a hotel.[23]

Korte Voorhout in The Hague, the Netherlands
Early years of marriage

After Carolina and Charles Christian's marriage in 1760, they needed a residence in The Hague and they began buying properties in The Hague on the Nieuwe or Korte Voorhout. The building of an actual palace on the site would not begin until 1766. The architect they hired was Pieter de Swart, who had also worked for Carolina's father. He was also involved with plans for internal renovations for Huis ten Bosch and Korte Voorhout Palace would be his last major work. The move to Germany in 1769 effectively ended work on the new palace and when Pieter de Swart died in 1773, the main building was not even finished. More wings may have been in the works, but they were never started and so just the main building remains. It was divided into several rooms around the centre "cour", a billiard room, a bedroom, a cabinet, an antechamber, a music room, a dance hall and a reception room. After Charles Christian's death in 1788 the building and the surrounding grounds were sold for F35.000 – which was less than what Charles Christian had paid for it to be built. In 1799 it was transferred to the Batavian Republic and in 1804 it began its new life as a theatre, which is still in use today.[24]

Oude Gouvernement in Maastricht, The Netherlands
Official residence of the Governor of Maastricht

The residence in Maastricht initially existed of two separate mansions, which were expanded and renovated in the 17th and 18th century, also by Carolina's husband, Charles Christian, who was the Governor of Maastricht from 1772 until 1781. In 1777, architect Mathias Soiron improved the facade and added an entire new floor to the existing building. In 1803, Napoleon Bonaparte spent some time there. By 1927, the building was in such a state of disrepair that it was completely torn down and rebuilt in 1935 under the watchful eye of G.C Bremer, who also worked on the Peace Palace in The Hague. Until 1986, it housed the Limburg Provincial government. Since 1990, it is the home of the law faculty of the University of Maastricht.[25]

Castle Philippsruhe in Hanau, Germany
Mourning

After the tragic death of her son, William Louis, Carolina was, understandably, depressed for quite some time and per her husband's suggestion, she went to visit a friend of hers, the Landgravine of Hesse-Kassel at Castle Philippsruhe in Hanau. The Landgravine was not only her friend, but also her aunt.

The Castle Philippsruhe was actually not that old when Carolina visited it to take her mind of the death of her son. It was built between 1700 and 1725 by Count Philipp Reinhard of Hanau as a summer residence. A previous castle had been destroyed in the 30-year-war. The architect was Julius Ludwig Rothweil, who would later also work on Castle Arolsen. After just a year of construction he was replaced by the French architect Jacques Girard. The designs were based on the French castle of Clagny. It consists of a central building of two floors with living quarters with wings on either side with just one floor, which are centred around a courtyard. Upon Philipp Reinhard's death in 1712, the castle was inherited by his younger brother, Johann Reinhard. In 1723, an orangery was added to the north-west of the park. Johann Reinhard had a daughter named Charlotte, but no male heirs. By an inheritance contract the castle fell to the Hesse-Kassel line into the person of William VIII, Landgrave of Hesse-Kassel, Carolina's aunt's father-in-law.

The castle was caught up in the Austrian war of succession in 1743 and it housed troops for a little while. It wouldn't be the last time it would be caught in a war, as it also played a role in the Prussian Austrian War of 1806, the German French War of 1870/1871 and the First World War.[26] Despite this, the castle opened its doors in 1967 as the Historical Museum of Hanau. A fire in 1984 did some major damage to the rooms, but it was restored to its former glory.

References

Chapter 1

1. Schutte, Dr. G.J., *Oranje in de achttiende eeuw*, Buijten & Schipperheijn, Amsterdam, 1999 p. 49-50
2. Baker-Smith, Veronica P. M, *A Life of Anne of Hanover, Princess Royal*, Brill Academic Publishers, Leiden, 1995 p. 46
3. John Hervey, 2nd Baron Hervey was an English courtier and political writer
4. Hervey, John, 2nd Baron Hervey, *Memoirs of the Reign of George the Second*, John Murray, London, 1848, Volume 1 p. 271
5. Hervey, John, 2nd Baron Hervey, *Memoirs of the Reign of George the Second*, John Murray, London, 1848, Volume 1 p. 272
6. Arkell, Ruby Lillian Percival, *Caroline of Ansbach: George the Second's Queen*, Oxford University Press, London, 1939 p.212
7. Baker-Smith, Veronica P. M, *A Life of Anne of Hanover, Princess Royal*, Brill Academic Publishers, Leiden, 1995 p.53
8. K.H.A Willem IV, 171
9. K.H.A. Willem IV, 170 I
10. Ibid.
11. Arkell, Ruby Lillian Percival, *Caroline of Ansbach: George the Second's Queen*, Oxford University Press, London, 1939 p. 262
12. Baker-Smith, Veronica P. M, *A Life of Anne of Hanover, Princess Royal*, Brill Academic Publishers, Leiden, 1995 p.77
13. Quoted in Naber, Johanna W.A., *Carolina van Oranje*, H.D. Tjeenk Willink, Haarlem, 1910 p.8
14. K.H.A. Willem IV, 170 II
15. Ibid.
16. K.H.A Anna van Hanover, 430
17. Bentinck, Briefwisseling, Vol I, No CXXXVIII

18. Bentinck, Briefwisseling, Vol I, No CCXXXIX
19. K.H.A., Willem IV 170 III
20. Baker-Smith, Veronica P. M, *A Life of Anne of Hanover, Princess Royal*, Brill Academic Publishers, Leiden, 1995 p.99
21. Huizinga, J.J, *Van Leeuwarden naar Den Haag: Rond de verplaatoingon van het stadhouderlijke hof in 1747*, Van Wijnen, Franeker, 1997 p.37
22. Baker-Smith, Veronica P. M, *A Life of Anne of Hanover, Princess Royal*, Brill Academic Publishers, Leiden, 1995 p.107
23. Quoted in Naber, Johanna W.A., *Carolina van Oranje*, H.D. Tjeenk Willink, Haarlem, 1910 p.10
24. K.H.A Marie Louise of Hesse-Kassel, 15
25. Schreuder, Esther, *Cupido en Sideron*, Uitgeverij Balans, Amsterdam, 2017 p.21
26. Schreuder, Esther, *Cupido en Sideron*, Uitgeverij Balans, Amsterdam, 2017 p. 32
27. K.H.A.,Willem IV, 171
28. Ibid.
29. K.H.A., Willem IV, 33
30. Nijhoff, Dirk Christiaan, *De Hertog van Brunswijk: eene bijdrage tot de geschiedenis van Nederland gedurende de jaren 1750-1784*, 1889 p.216
31. Hardenbroek, Gijsbert Jan, *Gedenkschriften van Gijsbert Jan van Hardenbroek (1747-1787)*, J. Müller, 1903 p. 143
32. Naber, Johanna W.A., *Carolina van Oranje*, H.D. Tjeenk Willink, Haarlem, 1910 p.16
33. Freund ,Werner, *Mozart am Fürstenhof im Kirchheimbolanden*, Freund, Kirchheimbolanden, 1991 p. 74-75
34. Naber, Johanna W.A., *Carolina van Oranje*, H.D. Tjeenk Willink, Haarlem, 1910 p.16
35. Naber, Johanna W.A., *Carolina van Oranje*, H.D. Tjeenk Willink, Haarlem, 1910 p.17
36. Naber, Johanna W.A., *Carolina van Oranje*, H.D. Tjeenk Willink, Haarlem, 1910 p.18

37. Naber, Johanna W.A., *Carolina van Oranje*, H.D. Tjeenk Willink, Haarlem, 1910 p.19
38. Quoted in Naber, Johanna W.A., *Carolina van Oranje*, H.D. Tjeenk Willink, Haarlem, 1910 p.21
39. K.H.A, Anna van Hannover, 430
40. K.H.A. Anna van Hannover, 404
41. Jagtenberg, Fred, *Marijke Meu 1688 – 1765*, Uitgeverij Bornmeer, Gorredijk, 2015 p.278
42. K.H.A Marie Louise of Hesse-Kassel, 68
43. Quoted in Naber, Johanna W.A., *Carolina van Oranje*, H.D. Tjeenk Willink, Haarlem, 1910 p.24
44. Quoted in Naber, Johanna W.A., *Carolina van Oranje*, H.D. Tjeenk Willink, Haarlem, 1910 p.25
45. Naber, Johanna W.A., *Carolina van Oranje*, H.D. Tjeenk Willink, Haarlem, 1910 p.28
46. Quoted in Naber, Johanna W.A., *Carolina van Oranje*, H.D. Tjeenk Willink, Haarlem, 1910 p.29

Chapter 2
1. Naber, Johanna W.A., *Carolina van Oranje*, H.D. Tjeenk Willink, Haarlem, 1910 p.31
2. Naber, Johanna W.A., *Carolina van Oranje*, H.D. Tjeenk Willink, Haarlem, 1910 p.30
3. Naber, Johanna W.A., *Carolina van Oranje*, H.D. Tjeenk Willink, Haarlem, 1910 p.33
4. Naber, Johanna W.A., *Carolina van Oranje*, H.D. Tjeenk Willink, Haarlem, 1910 p. 35
5. K.H.A Willem V, 80
6. Naber, Johanna W.A., *Carolina van Oranje*, H.D. Tjeenk Willink, Haarlem, 1910 p.35
7. K.H.A Willem V, 80
8. K.H.A Marie Louise of Hesse-Kassel, 16
9. K.H.A Willem V, 80
10. Morren, Th., *Het Huis Honselaarsdijk*, 1904 p.80

11. Hardenbroek, Gijsbert Jan, *Gedenkschriften van Gijsbert Jan van Hardenbroek (1747-1787)*, J. Müller, 1903 p.147 and p. 249

12. K.H.A Willem V, 463

13. K.H.A Willem V, 463

14. K.H.A Willem V, 463

15. Kalff, S, *Karakters uit den pruikentijd – Maryke-Meu*, B. van de Watering, 1902 p.35

16. Schrader, J., *Epicedion Mariae Ludovicae*, 1765 p. 34-36

17. Chalmot, J.A de, *Afkomst, godvruchtig Leven en Zalig dood van Hare Doorluchtigste Hoogheid Maria Louise, Princesse Douairiere van Oranje en Nassau, geboren Landgravin van Hesse-Cassel etc etc*, 1765

18. Jagtenberg, Fred, *Marijke Meu 1688 – 1765*, Uitgeverij Bornmeer, Gorredijk, 2015 p. 344-345

19. K.H.A Willem V, 463

20. K.H.A Willem V, 463

21. K.H.A Willem V, 463

22. K.H.A Willem V, 463

23. K.H.A Willem V, 463

24. K.H.A Willem V, 463

25. Dearling, Robert, *The Music of Wolfgang Amadeus Mozart, the Symphonies*, Fairleigh Dickinson University Press, Madison, 1982 p.34

26. Mozart, Wolfgang Amadeus, *A life in letters*, Penguin Books, London, 2006 p.46-47

27. Freund ,Werner, *Mozart am Fürstenhof im Kirchheimbolanden*, Freund, Kirchheimbolanden, 1991 p.22

28. Freund ,Werner, *Mozart am Fürstenhof im Kirchheimbolanden*, Freund, Kirchheimbolanden, 1991 p.22

29. Naber, Johanna W.A., *Carolina van Oranje*, H.D. Tjeenk Willink, Haarlem, 1910 p. 44

30. Freund ,Werner, *Mozart am Fürstenhof im Kirchheimbolanden*, Freund, Kirchheimbolanden, 1991 p.29

31. Freund ,Werner, *Mozart am Fürstenhof im Kirchheimbolanden*,

Freund, Kirchheimbolanden, 1991 p.36

32. Freund ,Werner, *Mozart am Fürstenhof im Kirchheimbolanden*, Freund, Kirchheimbolanden, 1991 p.30
33. Freund ,Werner, *Mozart am Fürstenhof im Kirchheimbolanden*, Freund, Kirchheimbolanden, 1991 p.65

Chapter 3

1. Freund ,Werner, *Mozart am Fürstenhof im Kirchheimbolanden*, Freund, Kirchheimbolanden, 1991 p.54
2. Freund ,Werner, *Mozart am Fürstenhof im Kirchheimbolanden*, Freund, Kirchheimbolanden, 1991 p.57
3. Freund ,Werner, *Mozart am Fürstenhof im Kirchheimbolanden*, Freund, Kirchheimbolanden, 1991 p.59
4. Freund ,Werner, *Mozart am Fürstenhof im Kirchheimbolanden*, Freund, Kirchheimbolanden, 1991 p.59
5. Freund ,Werner, *Mozart am Fürstenhof im Kirchheimbolanden*, Freund, Kirchheimbolanden, 1991 p.61
6. Freund ,Werner, *Mozart am Fürstenhof im Kirchheimbolanden*, Freund, Kirchheimbolanden, 1991 p.61
7. Freund ,Werner, *Mozart am Fürstenhof im Kirchheimbolanden*, Freund, Kirchheimbolanden, 1991 p.61
8. Naber, Johanna W.A., *Carolina van Oranje*, H.D. Tjeenk Willink, Haarlem, 1910 p. 56
9. Naber, Johanna W.A., *Carolina van Oranje*, H.D. Tjeenk Willink, Haarlem, 1910 p. 59
10. Naber, Johanna W.A., *Carolina van Oranje*, H.D. Tjeenk Willink, Haarlem, 1910 p. 60
11. Naber, Johanna W.A., *Carolina van Oranje*, H.D. Tjeenk Willink, Haarlem, 1910 p. 60
12. Naber, Johanna W.A., *Carolina van Oranje*, H.D. Tjeenk Willink, Haarlem, 1910 p. 62
13. K.H.A Willem V, 463
14. K.H.A Willem V, 463
15. K.H.A Willem V, 463

16. K.H.A Willem V, 463
17. Naber, Johanna W.A., *Carolina van Oranje*, H.D. Tjeenk Willink, Haarlem, 1910 p. 66
18. Naber, Johanna W.A., *Carolina van Oranje*, H.D. Tjeenk Willink, Haarlem, 1910 p. 67
19. K.H.A Willem V, 463
20. K.H.A Willem V, 463
21. K.H.A Willem V, 463
22. K.H.A Willem V, 463
23. K.H.A Willem V, 463
24. K.H.A Willem V, 463
25. K.H.A Willem V, 463
26. K.H.A Willem V, 463
27. Naber, Johanna W.A., *Carolina van Oranje*, H.D. Tjeenk Willink, Haarlem, 1910 p. 74-75
28. K.H.A Willem V, 463
29. K.H.A Willem V, 463
30. K.H.A Willem V, 463
31. K.H.A Willem V, 463
32. K.H.A Willem V, 463
33. K.H.A Willem V, 463
34. Naber, Johanna W.A., *Carolina van Oranje*, H.D. Tjeenk Willink, Haarlem, 1910 p.82
35. K.H.A Willem V, 493
36. K.H.A Willem V, 493
37. Freund ,Werner, *Mozart am Fürstenhof im Kirchheimbolanden*, Freund, Kirchheimbolanden, 1991 p.130
38. Freund ,Werner, *Mozart am Fürstenhof im Kirchheimbolanden*, Freund, Kirchheimbolanden, 1991 p.132-133
39. Freund ,Werner, *Mozart am Fürstenhof im Kirchheimbolanden*, Freund, Kirchheimbolanden, 1991 p.130
40. K.H.A Willem V, 463
41. K.H.A Willem V, 493
42. Naber, Johanna W.A., *Carolina van Oranje*, H.D. Tjeenk

Willink, Haarlem, 1910 p.90
43. K.H.A Willem V, 463
44. K.H.A Willem V, 463
45. K.H.A Willem V, 493
46. K.H.A Willem V, 463
47. Naber, Johanna W.A., *Carolina van Oranje*, H.D. Tjeenk Willink, Haarlem, 1910 p.129
48. Naber, Johanna W.A., *Carolina van Oranje*, H.D. Tjeenk Willink, Haarlem, 1910 p.127-128
49. Naber, Johanna W.A., *Carolina van Oranje*, H.D. Tjeenk Willink, Haarlem, 1910 p.129
50. K.H.A Willem V, 463
51. K.H.A Willem V, 463
52. K.H.A Willem V, 463
53. K.H.A Willem V, 463
54. K.H.A Willem V, 463
55. Naber, Johanna W.A., *Carolina van Oranje*, H.D. Tjeenk Willink, Haarlem, 1910 p.152
56. K.H.A Willem V, 493
57. Heinel, Jürgen, *Die Seniorenresidenz Schloß Kirchheimbolanden und ihre fürstliche Herkunft*, Otterbach-Arbogast, Otterbach, 1995 p.40

Chapter 4

1. http://www.weilburg-lahn.info/pdf/biografie_karl_christian_lang.pdf accessed on 30 May 2017
2. Meerkerk, Edwin van,*Willem V en Wilhelmina van Pruisen*, Atlas-Contact, Amsterdam, 2009 p.84-86
3. Meerkerk, Edwin van,*Willem V en Wilhelmina van Pruisen*, Atlas-Contact, Amsterdam, 2009 p. 93-96
4. Meerkerk, Edwin van,*Willem V en Wilhelmina van Pruisen*, Atlas-Contact, Amsterdam, 2009 p. 118-132
5. Meerkerk, Edwin van,*Willem V en Wilhelmina van Pruisen*, Atlas-Contact, Amsterdam, 2009 p. 132-133

6. Meerkerk, Edwin van,*Willem V en Wilhelmina van Pruisen*, Atlas-Contact, Amsterdam, 2009 p. 177-180

7. Meerkerk, Edwin van,*Willem V en Wilhelmina van Pruisen*, Atlas-Contact, Amsterdam, 2009 p. 186

8. Meerkerk, Edwin van,*Willem V en Wilhelmina van Pruisen*, Atlas-Contact, Amsterdam, 2009 p. 198

9. https://www.denederlandsegrondwet.nl/9353000/1/ j9vvihlf299q0sr/vi7hh35h85yv accessed on 23-7-2017

Chapter 5

1. Huizinga, J.J, *Van Leeuwarden naar Den Haag: Rond de verplaatsingen van het stadhouderlijke hof in 1747*, Van Wijnen, Franeker, 1997 p. 62-63

2. Karstkarel, Drs. G.P, *Het Stadhouderlijk hof en Koninklijk paleis te Leeuwarden*, Vereniging Oranje-Nassau Museum, 's-Gravenhage, 1985

3. Mulder-Radetzky, R.L.P. and J.A. Mulder, *Museum het Princessehof*, Museum Het Princessehof , Leeuwarden, 1992

4. Haersma Buma, Bernard van, *Grote of Jacobijner Kerk te Leeuwarden*, Uitgeverij Kok ten Have, Utrecht, 2008

5. Mulder-Radetsky, Drs. R.L.P and B.H. De Vries, *Geschiedenis van Oranjewoud*, Canaletto, Alphen aan den Rijn, 1989 p. 7-12

6. Mulder-Radetsky, Drs. R.L.P and B.H. De Vries, *Geschiedenis van Oranjewoud*, Canaletto, Alphen aan den Rijn, 1989 p. 13-14

7. Mulder-Radetsky, Drs. R.L.P and B.H. De Vries, *Geschiedenis van Oranjewoud*, Canaletto, Alphen aan den Rijn, 1989 p. 20

8. Huizinga, J.J, *Van Leeuwarden naar Den Haag: Rond de verplaatsingen van het stadhouderlijke hof in 1747*, Van Wijnen, Franeker, 1997 p.35 – 36

9. Mulder-Radetsky, Drs. R.L.P and B.H. De Vries, *Geschiedenis van Oranjewoud*, Canaletto, Alphen aan den Rijn, 1989 p. 93

10. Valk Bouman, J.M. Van der, *'t Konings Loo*, Nijgh Versluys, Baarn, 1985

11. Schmidt, F.H., *Pieter de Swart. Architect van de achttiende eeuw*, Uitgeverij Wbooks, Zwolle, 1999 p.83

12. Alberts, Jaco et al, *Het Haagse Binnenhof. Acht eeuwen centrum van macht*, Prodemos, The Hague, 2013

13. Loonstra, Marten, *The Royal Palace Huis ten Bosch in a historical view*, Walburg Pers, Zutphen, 1985

14. Jansen, Mieke et al, *Paleis Soestdijk. Drie eeuwen huis van Oranje*, Uitgeverij W Books B.V, Zwolle, 2009 p.21

15. Jansen, Mieke et al, *Paleis Soestdijk. Drie eeuwen huis van Oranje*, Uitgeverij W Books B.V, Zwolle, 2009

16. Naber, Johanna W.A., *Carolina van Oranje*, H.D. Tjeenk Willink, Haarlem, 1910 p.31

17. http://www.grotekerkdenhaag.nl accessed on 14 June 2017

18. Morren, Th., *Het Huis Honselaarsdijk*, 1904 p.75-80

19. Morren, Th., *Het Huis Honselaarsdijk*, 1904 p.80

20. Heinel, Jürgen, *Die Seniorenresidenz Schloß Kirchheimbolanden und ihre fürstliche Herkunft*, Otterbach-Arbogast, Otterbach, 1995 p. 13-23

21. Heinel, Jürgen, *Die Seniorenresidenz Schloß Kirchheimbolanden und ihre fürstliche Herkunft*, Otterbach-Arbogast, Otterbach, 1995 p. 29-41

22. Heinel, Jürgen, *Die Seniorenresidenz Schloß Kirchheimbolanden und ihre fürstliche Herkunft*, Otterbach-Arbogast, Otterbach, 1995 p. 42-54

23. Olschewski, Eckhard, *Schloss und Schlossgarten Weilburg/Lahn*, Staatliche Schlösser unt Gärten Hessen, Seligenstadt, 2001

24. Slechte, C.H., G. Verstraete and L. van der Zalm, *175 Jaar Koninklijke Schouwburg 1804 – 1979*, Krusemann, 's-Gravenhage, 1979 p.13-19

25. Ubachs, Pierre and Ingrid Evers, *Historische Encyclopedie Maastricht*, Walburg Pers, Zutphen, 2005 p.201

26. Hoffmann, Klaus, *Schloss Philippsruhe: vom Barockschloss zum Historischen Museum*, CoCon, Hanau, 2001

Bibliography

Alberts, Jaco et al, *Het Haagse Binnenhof. Acht eeuwen centrum van macht*, Prodemos, The Hague, 2013

Arkell, Ruby Lillian Percival, *Caroline of Ansbach: George the Second's Queen*, Oxford University Press, London, 1939

Bentinck, *Briefwisseling, Vol I, No CXXXVIII*, N. Japikse, 1927-1935

Bentinck, *Briefwisseling, Vol I, No CCXXXIX*, N. Japikse, 1927-1935

Baker-Smith, Veronica P. M, *A Life of Anne of Hanover, Princess Royal*, Brill Academic Pub, Leiden, 1995

de Chalmot, J.A, *Afkomst, godvruchtig Leven en Zalig dood van Hare Doorluchtigste Hoogheid Maria Louise, Princesse Douairiere van Oranje en Nassau, geboren Landgravin van Hesse-Cassel etc etc*, 1765

Dearling, Robert, *The Music of Wolfgang Amadeus Mozart, the Symphonies*, Fairleigh Dickinson University Press, Madison, 1982

Freund ,Werner, *Mozart am Fürstenhof im Kirchheimbolanden*, Freund, Kirchheimbolanden, 1991

Haersma Buma, Bernard van, *Grote of Jacobijner Kerk te Leeuwarden*, Uitgeverij Kok ten Have, Utrecht, 2008

Hardenbroek, Gijsbert Jan, *Gedenkschriften van Gijsbert Jan van Hardenbroek (1747-1787)*, J. Müller, 1903

Heinel, Jürgen, *Die Seniorenresidenz Schloß Kirchheimbolanden und ihre fürstliche Herkunft*, Otterbach-Arbogast, Otterbach, 1995

Hervey, John, 2nd Baron Hervey, *Memoirs of the Reign of George the Second*, John Murray, London, 1848

Hoffmann, Klaus, *Schloss Philippsruhe: vom Barockschloss zum Historischen Museum*, CoCon, Hanau, 2001

Huizinga, J.J, *Van Leeuwarden naar Den Haag: Rond de verplaatsingen van het stadhouderlijke hof in 1747*, Van Wijnen, Franeker, 1997

Jagtenberg, Fred, *Marijke Meu 1688 – 1765*, Uitgeverij Bornmeer, Gorredijk, 2015

Jansen, Mieke et al, *Paleis Soestdijk. Drie eeuwen huis van Oranje*, Uitgeverij W Books B.V, Zwolle, 2009

Kalff, S, *Karakters uit den pruikentijd – Maryke-Meu*, B. van de Watering, 1902

Karstkarel, Drs. G.P, *Het Stadhouderlijk hof en Koninklijk paleis te Leeuwarden*, Vereniging Oranje-Nassau Museum, 's-Gravenhage, 1985

Loonstra, Marten, *The Royal Palace Huis ten Bosch in a historical view*, Walburg Pers, Zutphen, 1985

Meerkerk, Edwin van,*Willem V en Wilhelmina van Pruisen*, Atlas-Contact, Amsterdam, 2009

Morren, Th., *Het Huis Honselaarsdijk*, 1904

Mozart, Wolfgang Amadeus, *A life in letters*, Penguin Books, London, 2006

Mulder-Radetsky, Drs. R.L.P and B.H. De Vries, *Geschiedenis van Oranjewoud*, Canaletto, Alphen aan den Rijn, 1989

Mulder-Radetzky, R.L.P. and J.A. Mulder, *Museum het Princessehof*, Museum Het Princessehof , Leeuwarden, 1992

Naber, Johanna W.A., *Carolina van Oranje*, H.D. Tjeenk Willink, Haarlem, 1910

Nijhoff, Dirk Christiaan, *De Hertog van Brunswijk: eene bijdrage tot de geschiedenis van Nederland gedurende de jaren 1750-1784*, 1889

Olschewski, Eckhard, *Schloss und Schlossgarten Weilburg/Lahn*, Staatliche Schlösser unt Gärten Hessen, Seligenstadt, 2001

Schmidt, F.H., *Pieter de Swart. Architect van de achttiende eeuw*, Uitgeverij Wbooks, Zwolle, 1999

Schrader, J., *Epicedion Mariae Ludovicae*, 1765

Schreuder, Esther, *Cupido en Sideron*, Uitgeverij Balans, Amsterdam, 2017

Schutte, Dr. G.J., *Oranje in de achttiende eeuw*, Buijten & Schipperheijn, Amsterdam, 1999

Slechte, C.H., G. Verstraete and L. van der Zalm, *175 Jaar Koninklijke Schouwburg 1804 – 1979*, Krusemann, 's-Gravenhage, 1979

Ubachs, Pierre and Ingrid Evers, *Historische Encyclopedie Maastricht*, Walburg Pers, Zutphen, 2005

Valk Bouman, J.M. Van der, *'t Konings Loo*, Nijgh Versluys, Baarn, 1985

Royal archives
K.H.A Anna van Hanover
K.H.A Marie Louise of Hesse-Kassel
K.H.A Willem IV
K.H.A Willem V

Internet
http://www.weilburg-lahn.info/pdf/biografie_karl_christian_lang.pdf
https://www.denederlandsegrondwet.nl/9353000/1/j9vvihlf299q0sr/vi7hh35h85yv

Selected Index

Photos

1. Anne of Hanover - Rijkmuseum Amsterdam SK-A-406
2. William IV, Prince of Orange - Paleis Het Loo, Apeldoorn
3. George II of Great Britain - © National Portrait Gallery, London
4. Caroline of Ansbach - Warwickshire County Council
5. Arrival in Amsterdam – Rijksmuseum Amsterdam RP-P-OB-83.874
6. Carolina of Orange-Nassau – Rijksmuseum Amsterdam RP-P-OB-104.914
7. Anne of Hanover, William V, Prince of Orange and Carolina ot Orange-Nassau – Rijkmuseum Amsterdam RP-P-OB-104.914
8. William V, Prince of Orange – Mauritshuis Den Haag
9. Death of Anne of Hanover - Rijkmuseum Amsterdam RP-P-OB-84.513
10. Marriage of Carolina of Orange-Nassau and Charles Christian of Nassau-Weilburg - Rijkmuseum Amsterdam RP-P-1944-2048
11. Baptism of Carolina's first son - Rijksmuseum Amsterdam RP-P-OB-84.558
12. Carolina of Orange-Nassau and her children - Mauritshuis Den Haag
13. Carolina of Orange-Nassau – Rijksmuseum Amsterdam RP-T-00-1814 (also cover image)

Chronos Books
HISTORY

Chronos Books is an historical non-fiction imprint. Chronos
publishes real history for real people; bringing to life people,
places and events in an imaginative, easy-to-digest and
accessible way - histories that pass on their stories to a
generation of new readers.
If you have enjoyed this book, why not tell other readers by
posting a review on your preferred book site.

Recent bestsellers from Chronos Books are:

Lady Katherine Knollys
The Unacknowledged Daughter of King Henry VIII
Sarah-Beth Watkins
A comprehensive account of Katherine Knollys' questionable
paternity, her previously unexplored life in the Tudor court
and her intriguing relationship with Elizabeth I.
Paperback: 978-1-78279-585-8 ebook: 978-1-78279-584-1

Cromwell was Framed
Ireland 1649
Tom Reilly
Revealed: The definitive research that proves the Irish nation
owes Oliver Cromwell a huge posthumous apology for
wrongly convicting him of civilian atrocities in 1649.
Paperback: 978-1-78279-516-2 ebook: 978-1-78279-515-5

Why The CIA Killed JFK and Malcolm X
The Secret Drug Trade in Laos
John Koerner
A new groundbreaking work presenting evidence that the CIA
silenced JFK to protect its secret drug trade in Laos.
Paperback: 978-1-78279-701-2 ebook: 978-1-78279-700-5

The Disappearing Ninth Legion
A Popular History
Mark Olly
The Disappearing Ninth Legion examines hard evidence for the
foundation, development, mysterious disappearance, or possi-
ble continuation of Rome's lost Legion.
Paperback: 978-1-84694-559-5 ebook: 978-1-84694-931-9

Beaten But Not Defeated
Siegfried Moos - A German anti-Nazi who settled in Britain
Merilyn Moos
Siegi Moos, an anti-Nazi and active member of the German
Communist Party, escaped Germany in 1933 and, exiled in
Britain, sought another route to the transformation
of capitalism.
Paperback: 978-1-78279-677-0 ebook: 978-1-78279-676-3

A Schoolboy's Wartime Letters
An evacuee's life in WWII — A Personal Memoir
Geoffrey Iley
A boy writes home during WWII, revealing his own fascinating
story, full of zest for life, information and humour.
Paperback: 978-1-78279-504-9 ebook: 978-1-78279-503-2

The Life & Times of the Real Robyn Hoode
Mark Olly
A journey of discovery. The chronicles of the genuine historical
character, Robyn Hoode, and how he became one of England's
greatest legends.
Paperback: 978-1-78535-059-7 ebook: 978-1-78535-060-3

Readers of ebooks can buy or view any of these bestsellers by
clicking on the live link in the title. Most titles are published in
paperback and as an ebook. Paperbacks are available in
traditional bookshops. Both print and ebook formats are
available online.
Find more titles and sign up to our readers' newsletter at
http://www.johnhuntpublishing.com/history-home
Follow us on Facebook at
https://www.facebook.com/ChronosBooks
and Twitter at https://twitter.com/ChronosBooks